CD Track Listing and Song/Photo Index

Track #	Song Title	Photo Reference
1.	The Walls of Dùn Formna	pg. 23
2.	Roundstone Bay	pg. 47
3.	The Road to Galway	pg. 19
4.	The Patron Saint of Ballyvourney	pg. 24
5.	The Monastery at Kilmacduagh	pg. 56
6.	The Stone Table Dance	pg. 40
7.	Water Horses / At the Cliffs of Moher	pg. 11
8.	The Old Castle	pg. 7
9.	Twilight at Dunguaire	pg. 63
10.	The Plassy Shipwreck	pg. 27
11.	The Monastery at Kilmacduagh (reprise)	pg. 56

All Songs composed and arranged by John Mock
Kinvara Music (admin. by Murrah-Rich-Baierle)(BMI)

Celtic Portraits

Photography, Text, and Original Music by
John Mock

Additional Text Compiled By
Greg Howard

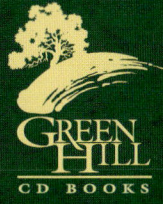

GREEN HILL
CD BOOKS

Edited by Greg Howard
Photography © 1998 John Mock
Art Direction: Andy Norris, Powell Creative Group
Design: Ian Black, Powell Creative Group
Printed by Harris Press

All rights reserved. No part of this book may be reproduced or utilized in any form or by any means, electronic or mechanical, photocopying, recording or any information and retrieval system without permission in writing from Green Hill Productions.

ISBN 0-9663601-0-9

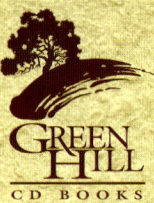

Green Hill
CD Books

Copyright ℗ © MCMXCVIII Green Hill Productions, a div. of Spring Hill Music Group, Inc.,
2021 Richard Jones Road, Ste. 180, Nashville, TN, 37215. All rights reserved.

Preface

I first visited Ireland in 1988. I was traveling with country singer Kathy Mattea and our schedule was busy enough that we had only a limited amount of time to see the country. However, it left an impression on me and I wanted to return there someday.

I was unable to travel there again until 1996. By that time I was playing a great deal of traditional Irish music and it had become a big influence in both my solo and orchestral writing. My wife, Lee, insisted I take her "point and shoot" camera despite my protests. I had never been one for taking pictures. By the end of my ten day trip I was hooked - not only on Ireland but on the idea of learning photography as well. I took a class, bought Ansel Adams books and began to study.

One year later, I was given the opportunity by Green Hill to record a project of original compositions depicting the countryside of Ireland. I had written some of these pieces in previous years, but most were composed in the summer of 1997, specifically for this recording. It was then that I started planning my third trip to Ireland. I wanted to shoot better photographs of the places I had visited earlier and written music about, as well as find new inspiration.

The combination of all of this became CELTIC PORTRAITS; musical composition and photography combined to give a "portrait" of Ireland, or perhaps it would be more honest to say a portrait of what my experience of Ireland has been so far.

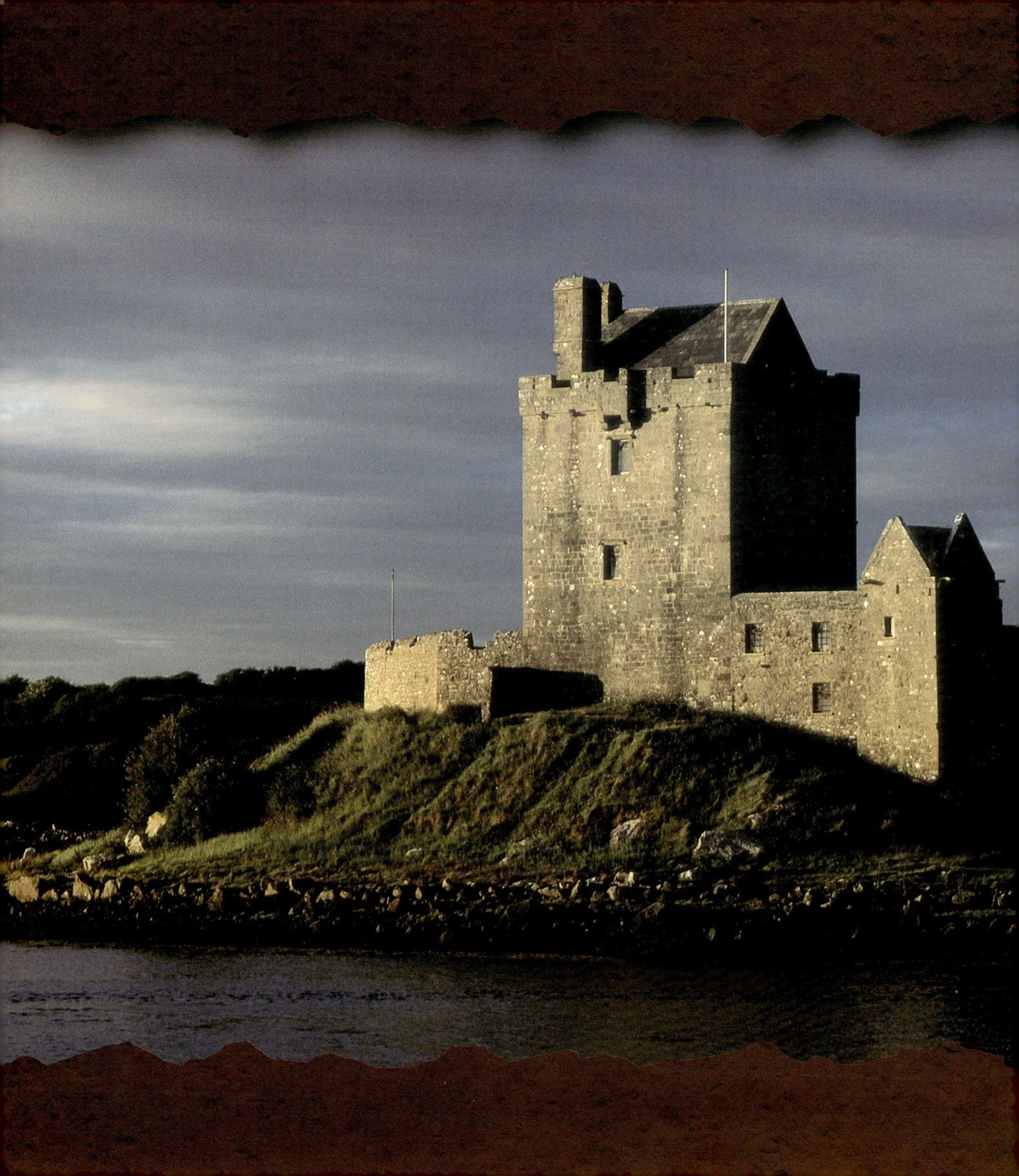

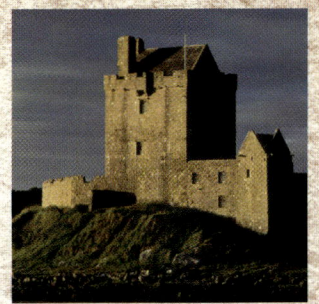

Dunguaire Castle in Kinvara, Co. Galway

The castle was built in 1510 and is named after Guaire, the 7th century King of Connacht. Due to the fact that Kilmacduagh monastery, with its monastic treasures, was situated only ten miles to the south, Kinvara was subject to frequent raids by the Vikings seeking access to the area through Kinvara bay. These raids would end when Brian Boru defeated the Viking power in 1014 A.D.

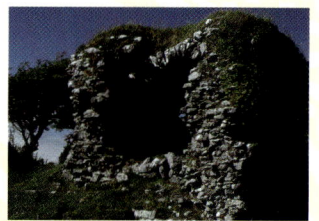

The Old Castle

Known simply as "The Old Castle" this ruin sits just to the west of Dunguaire Castle and is considerably older. Possibly, it was an ancient stronghold of an early Connacht settlement.

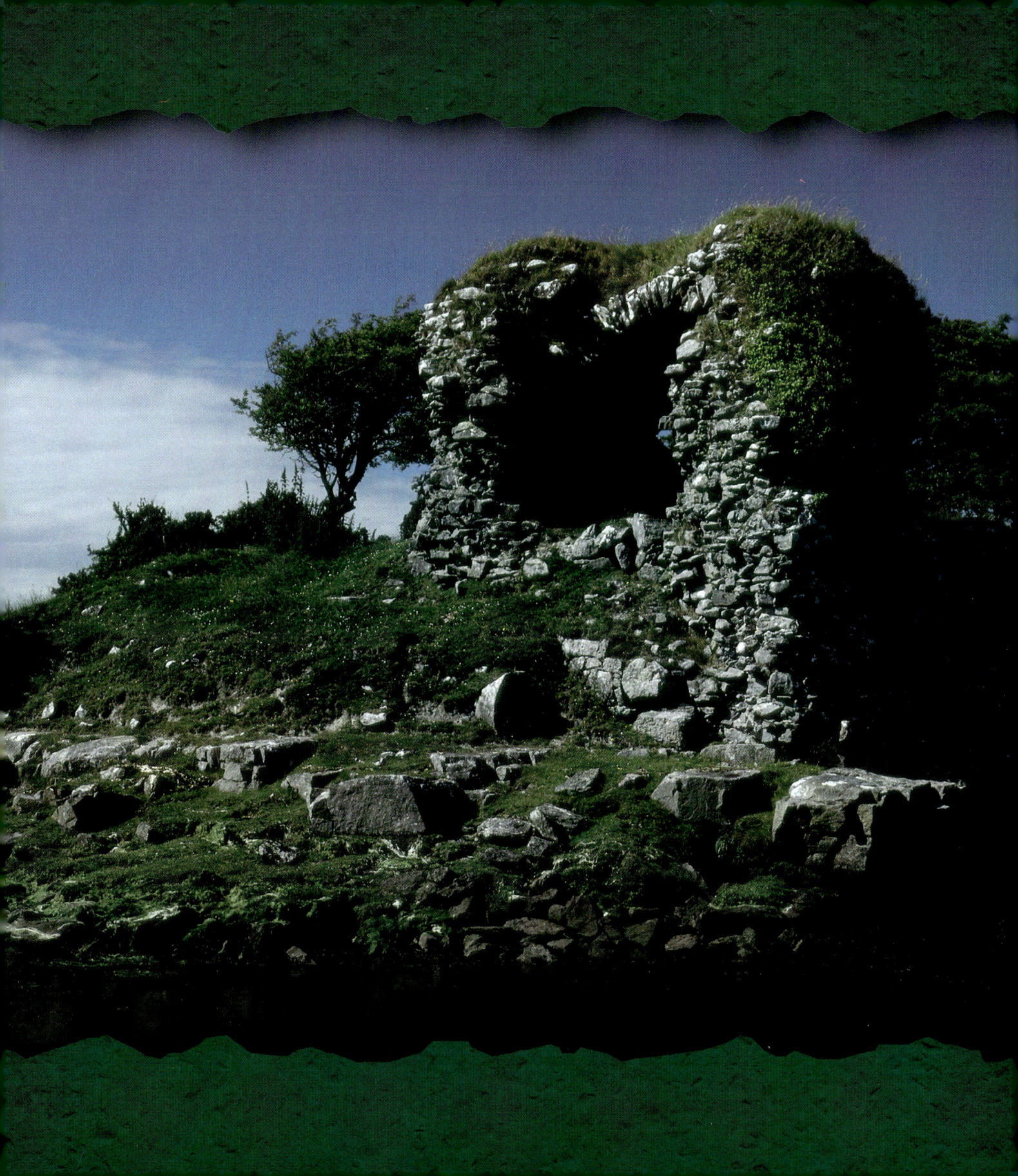

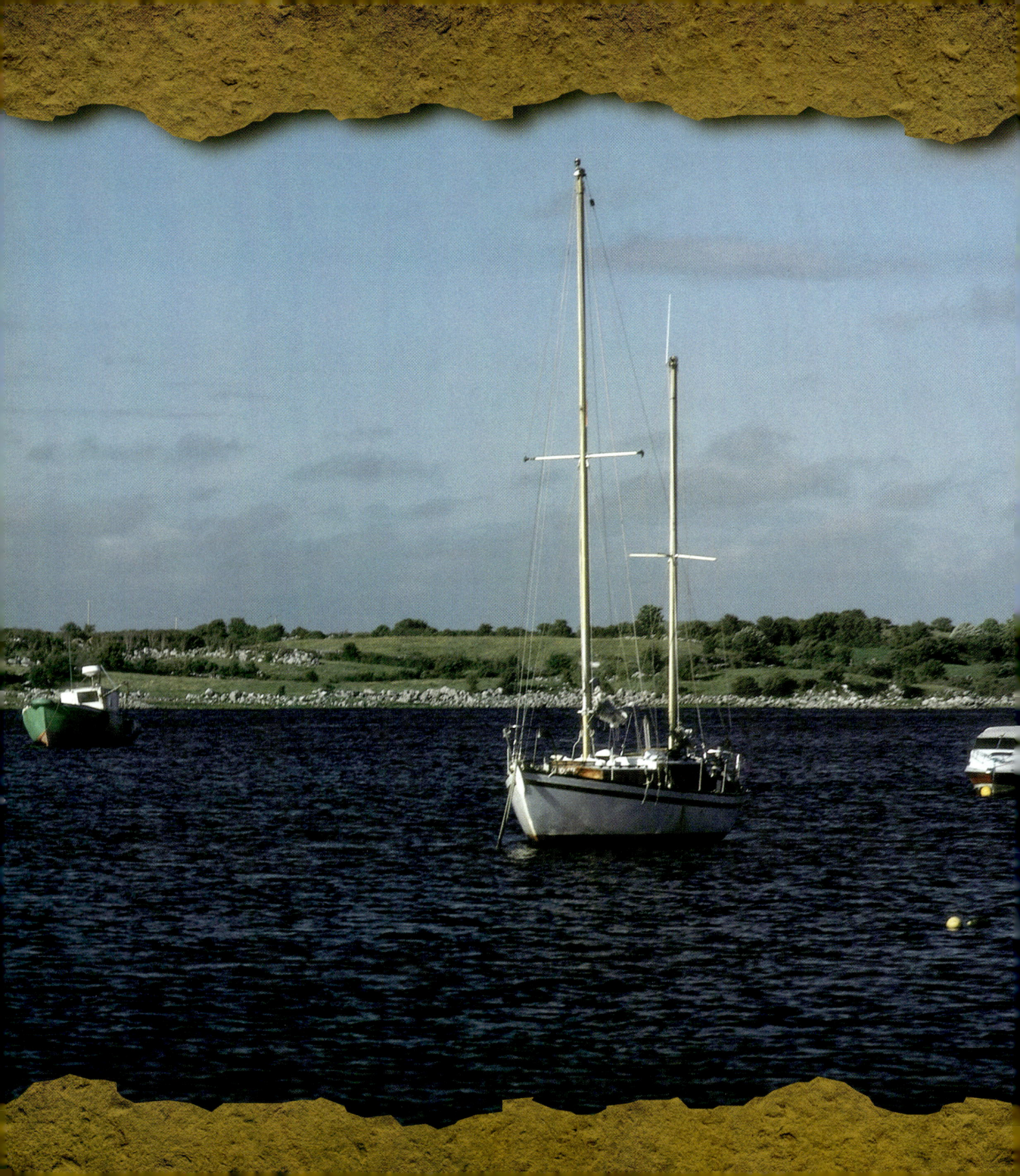

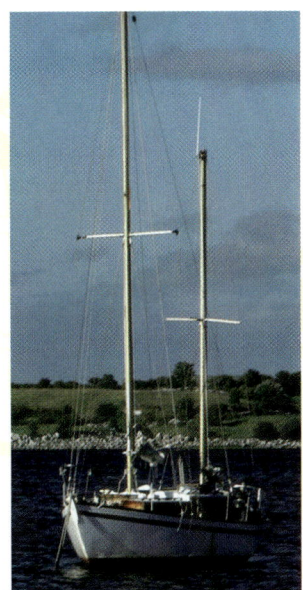

Kinvara

It is believed that at one time what would become Kinvara consisted of only a few small settlements. These settlements eventually developed into an important seaport town and upon realizing the area's potential, merchants soon began settling here.

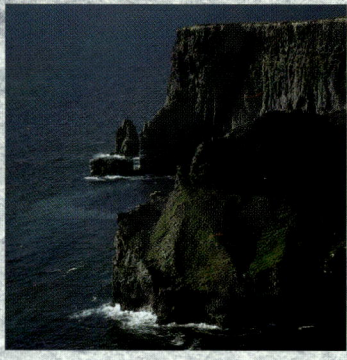

On some island I long to be,
a rocky promontory, looking on
the coiling surface of the sea.

To see the waves, crest on crest
of the great shining ocean, composing
a hymn to the creator, without rest.

To see without sadness the strand
lined with bright shells, and birds
lamenting overhead, a lonely sound.

To hear the whisper of small waves
against the rocks, that endless
sea sound, like keening over graves.

To watch the sea-birds sailing
in flocks, and most marvellous
of monsters, the turning whale.

To see the shift from ebbtide
to flood and tell my secret name:
'He who set his back on Ireland.

Colmcille
6th century

The Cliffs of Moher on the west coast of Clare

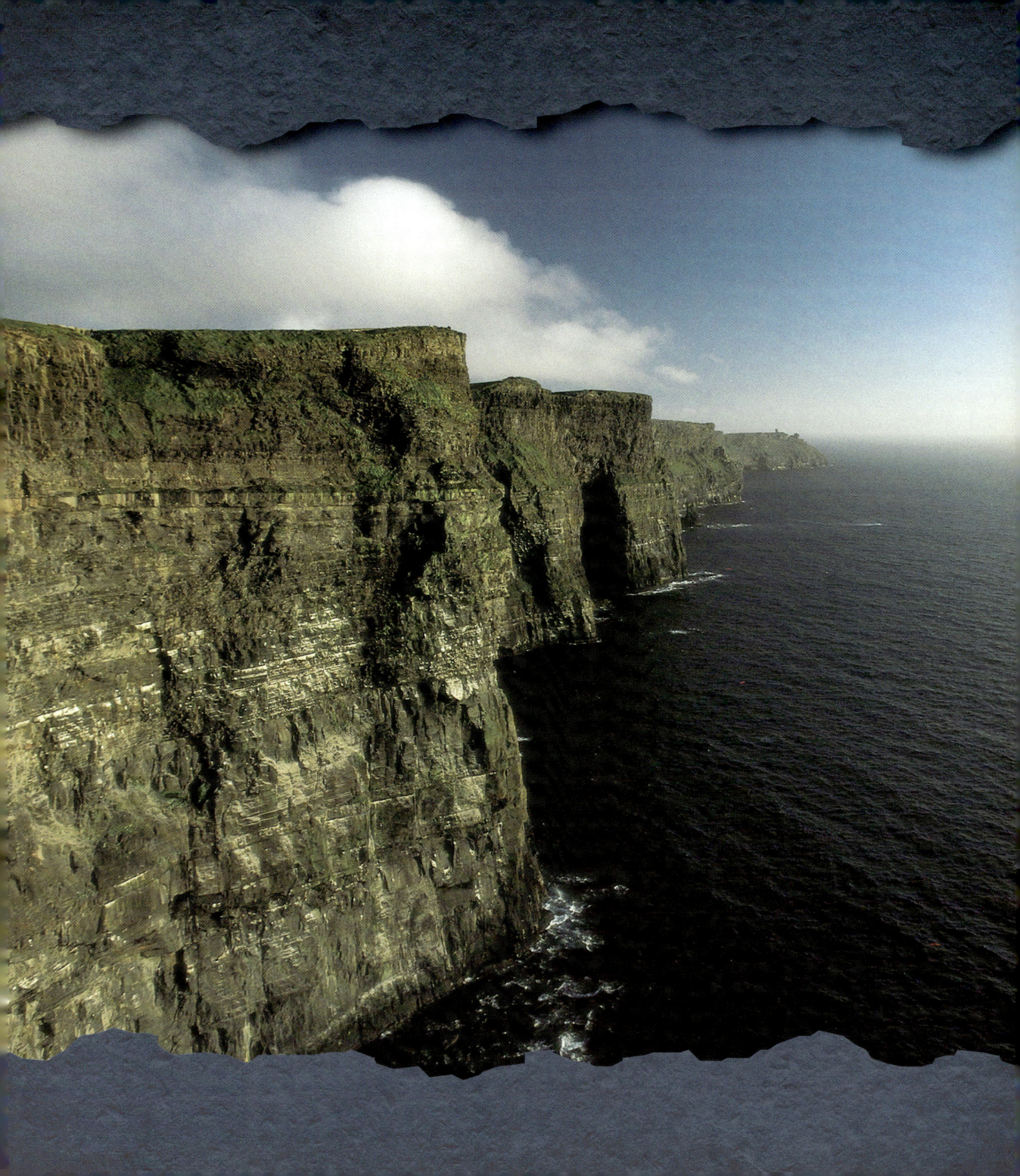

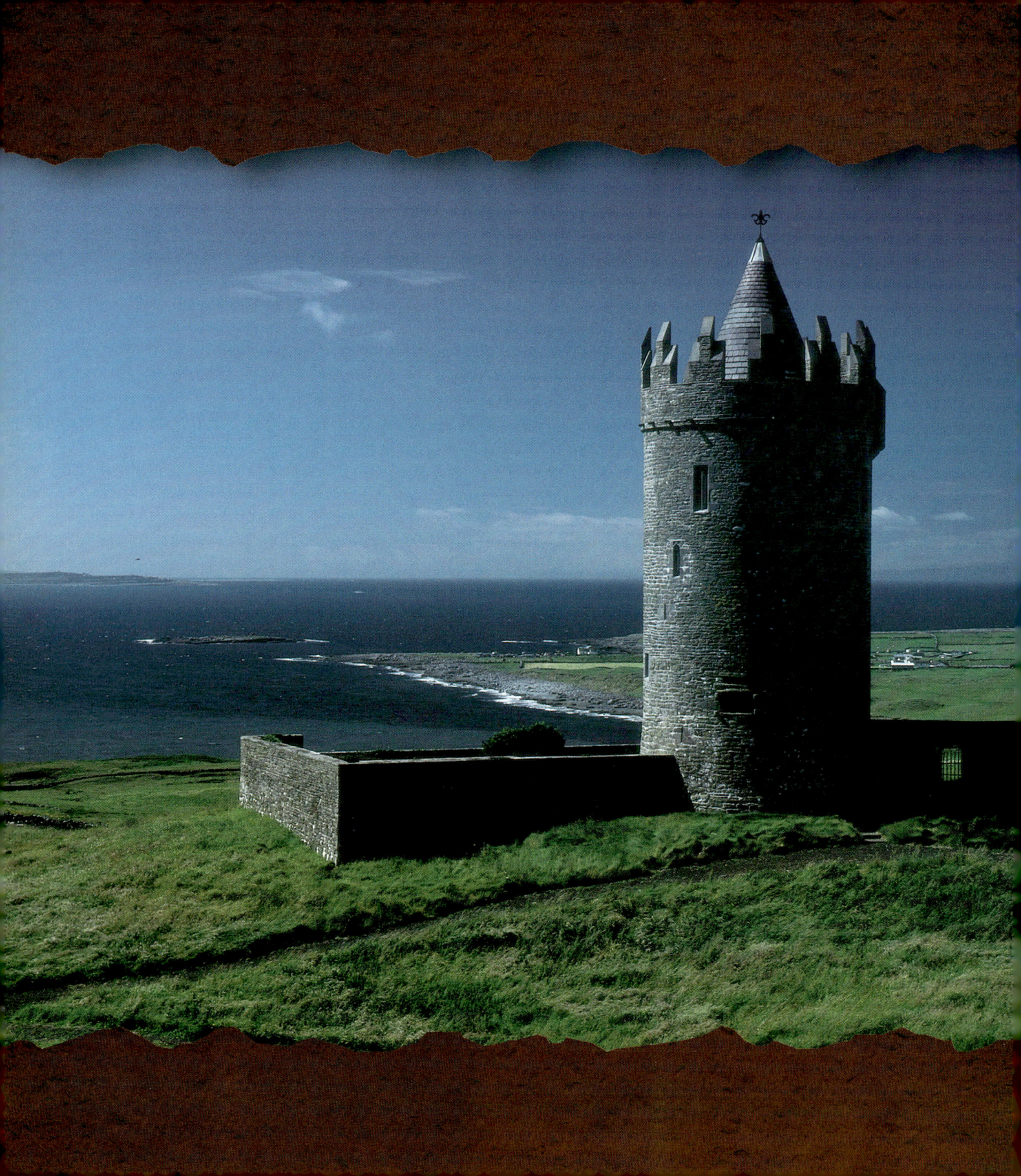

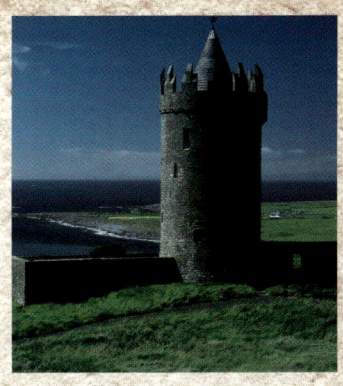

It is a pleasure to stand upon the shore, and to see ships tost upon the sea: a pleasure to stand in the window of a castle, and to see a battle and the adventures thereof below: but no pleasure is comparable to the standing upon the vantage ground of truth...and to see the errors, and wanderings, and mists, and tempests, in the vale below.

Francis Bacon
1625

Doonagore Castle in Doolin, Co. Clare

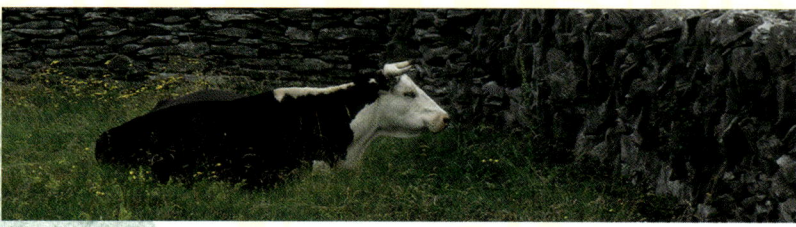

Aran Islands

In the far west of Ireland, across the mouth of Galway Bay, lie the Aran Islands. The three main islands are Inishmore (big island), Inishmaan (middle island) and Inishere (eastern island).

Legend as well as geology indicate that at one time the islands were connected to the mainland, with a large lake by the name of Loch Lurgan centered between them.

The Aran Islands are thought to be an extension of the Burren, and the similarity in the landscape can easily be seen.

An extraordinary wealth of ancient monuments can be found on these islands and a considerable amount of time can be spent exploring them. These islands have also provided inspiration for world famous writers such as J. M. Synge, Lady Gregory and James Joyce.

From this view point on Inishere, the island of Inishmaan can be seen in the distance.

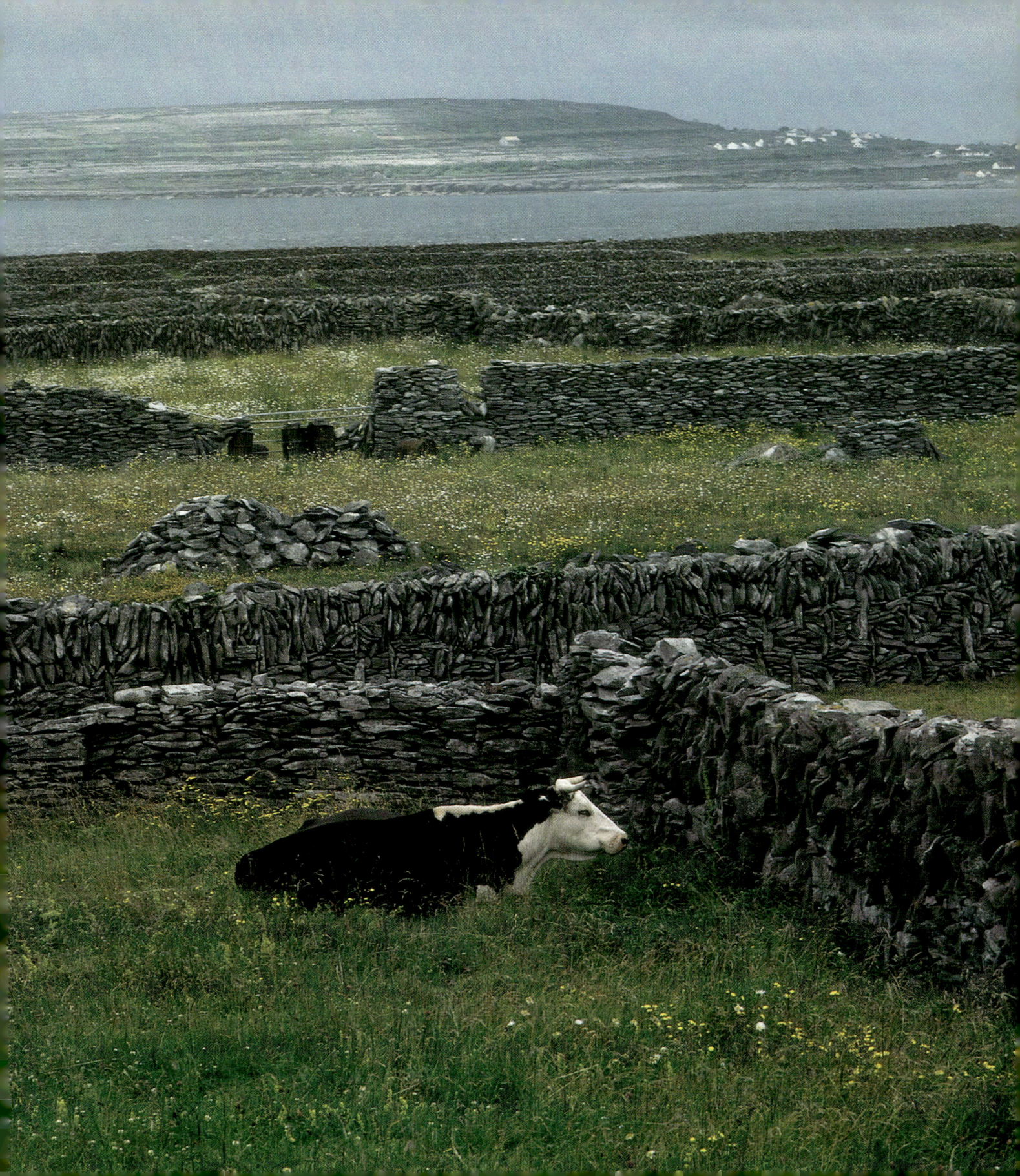

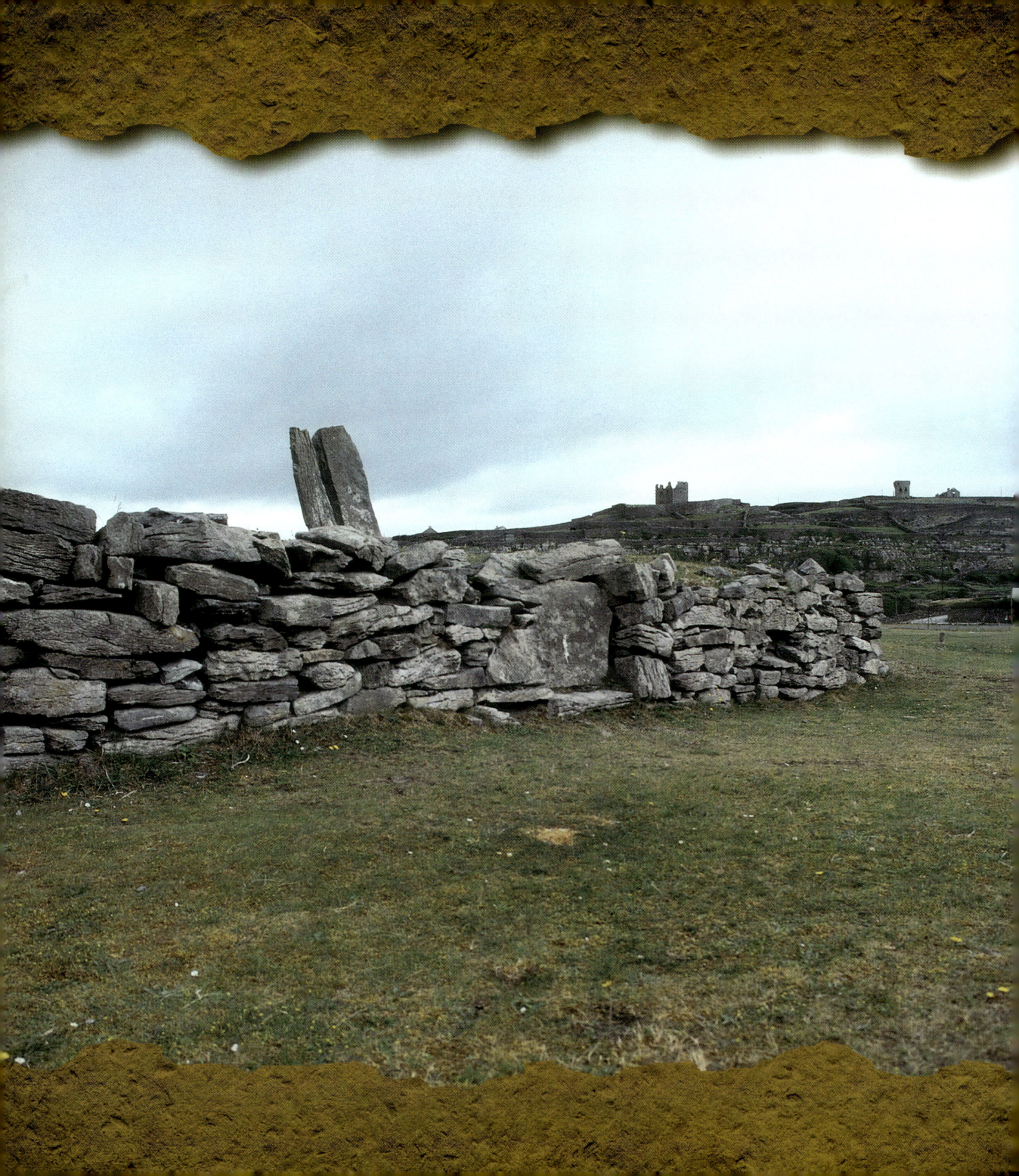

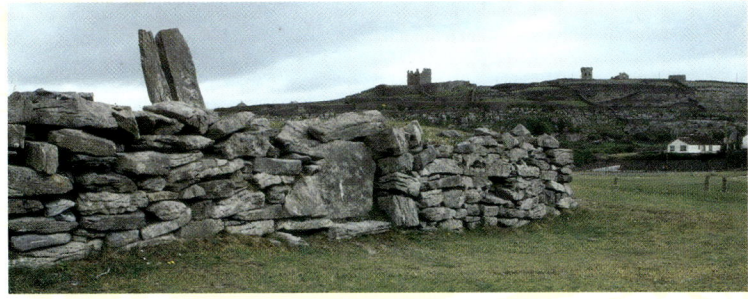

Cnoc Raithaí

This ancient burial sight can be found on Inishere. Excavated from the sight were two urns containing cremated bone. The larger of these urns dates back to 1,500 years B.C.

The first evidence of human habitation of the islands dates back to 2,500 B.C. and it is possible that people could have arrived as early as 4,000 B.C. These early settlers built stone tombs to hold the remains of their ancestors and many of these ancient tombs have survived to this day.

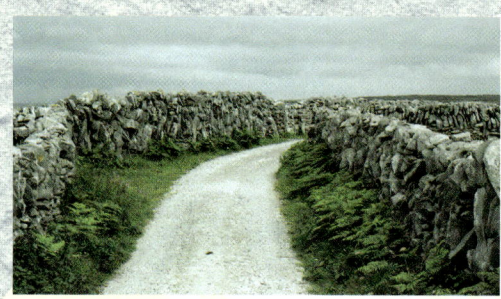

Prelude

Still south I went and west and south again,
Through Wicklow from the morning till the night,
And far from cities, and the sights of men,
Lived with the sunshine, and the moon's delight

I knew the stars, the flowers, and the birds,
the grey and wintry sides of many glens,
And did but half remember human words,
In converse with the mountains, moors, and fens.

J.M. Synge
(1871-1909)

A Road on the Island of Inishere, Co. Galway

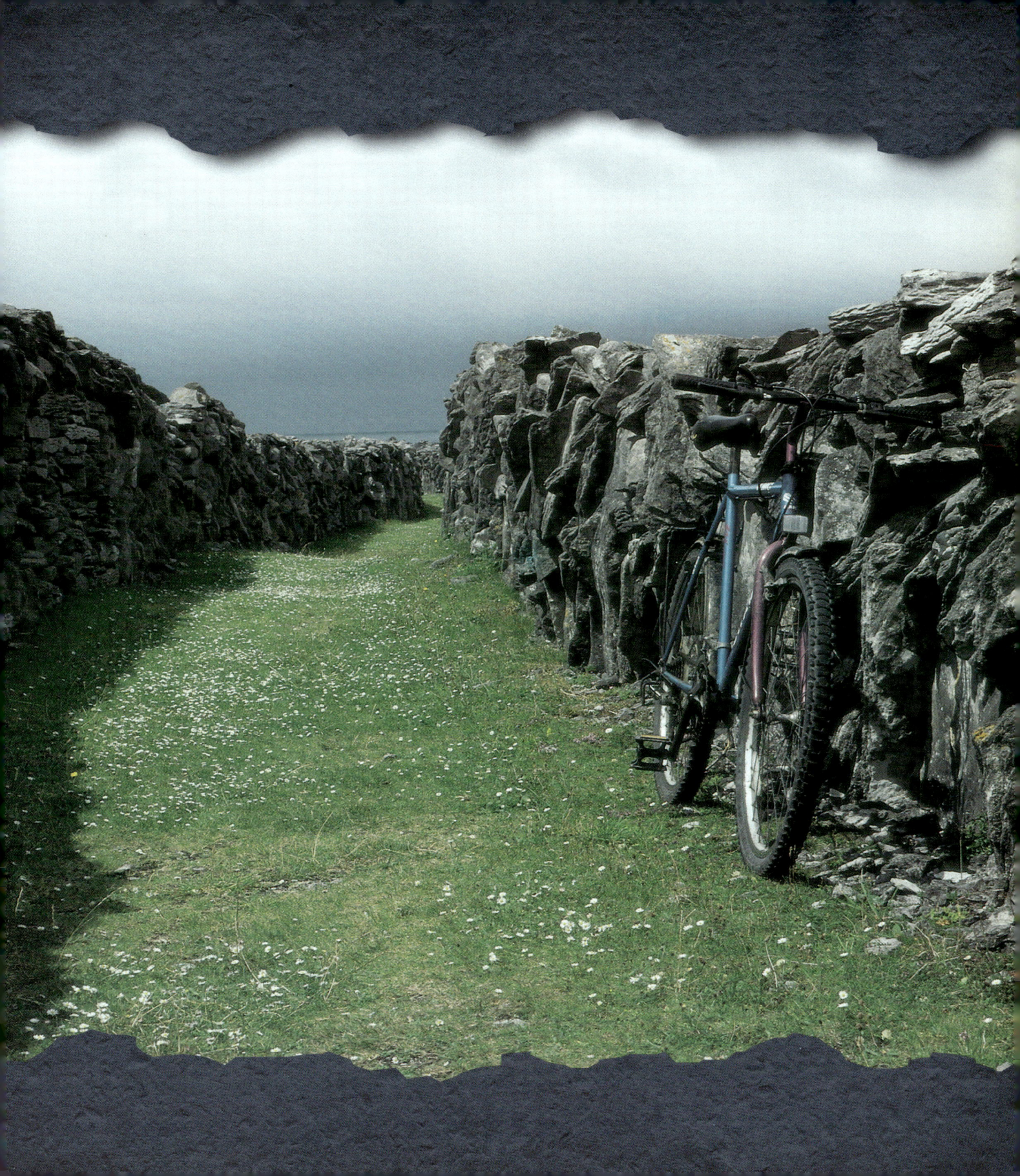

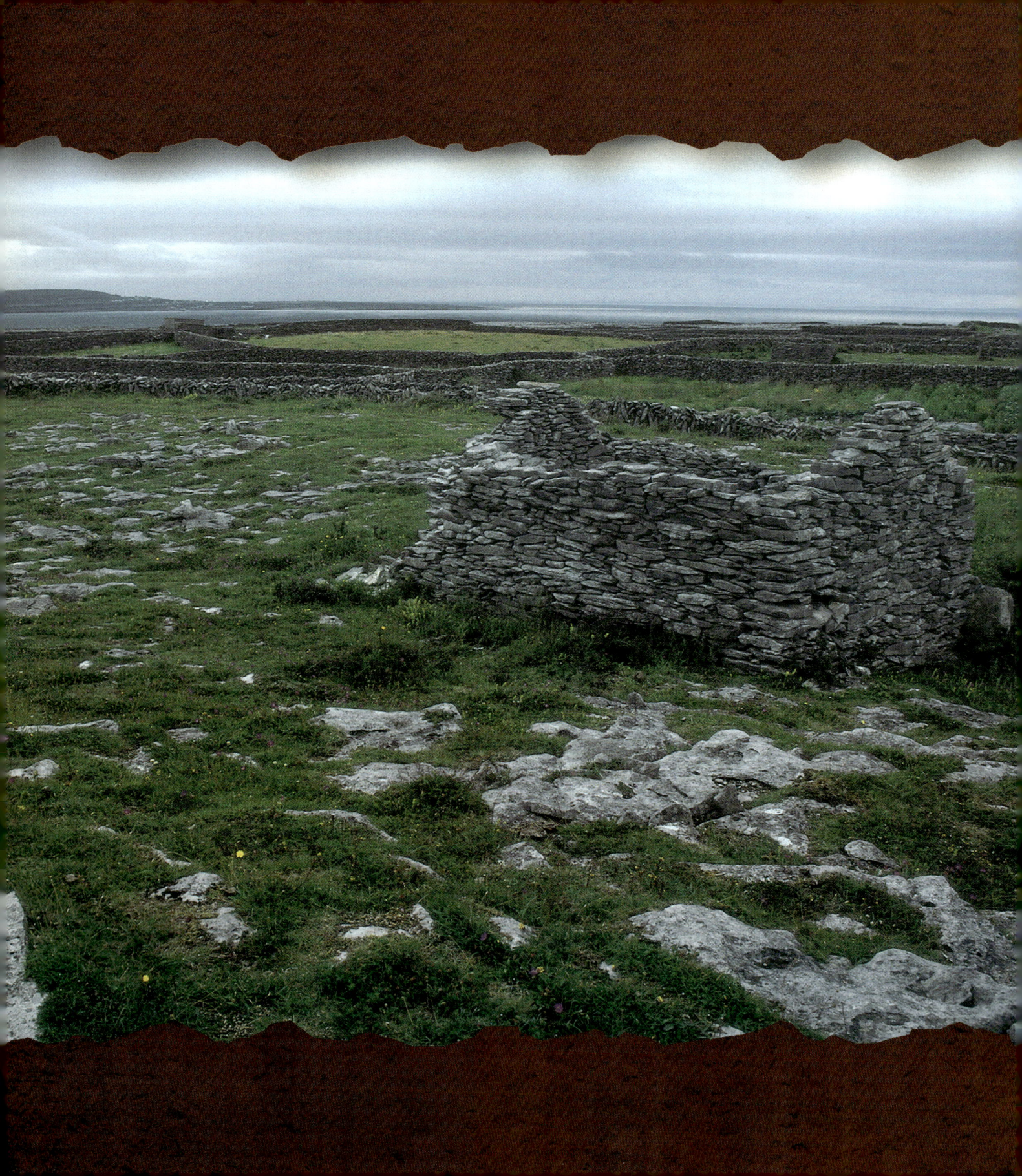

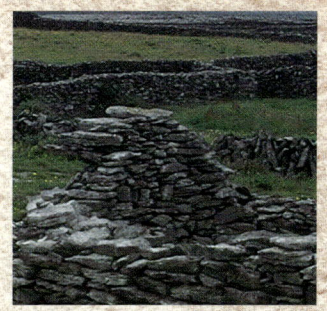

To an Isle in the Water

Shy one, Shy one,
Shy one of my heart,
She moves in the firelight
pensively apart,
She carries in the dishes,
And lays them in a row.
To an isle in the water
With her would I go.

With catries in the candles,
And lights the curtained room,
Shy in the doorway
And shy in the gloom;
And shy as a rabbit,
Helpful and shy.
To an isle in the water
With her would I fly.

William Butler Yeats
(1865-1939)

The abundance of rock and broken limestone found on these islands would become suitable building material for early inhabitants. This practice has continued through the centuries.

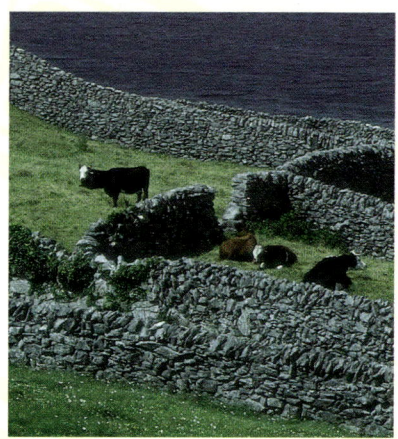

O'Brien's Castle

When looking for a site upon which to build a stronghold, defenders have historically chosen a natural strategic area, usually a hill, which could be easily defended.

Such is the case with 15th century O'Briens Castle. This castle on Inishere was built within the walls of an earlier stone fort by the name of Dún Formna. An ancient battle axe head dating from around 800 B.C. found buried here lends support to the idea that Dún Formna was the site of many bloody battles.

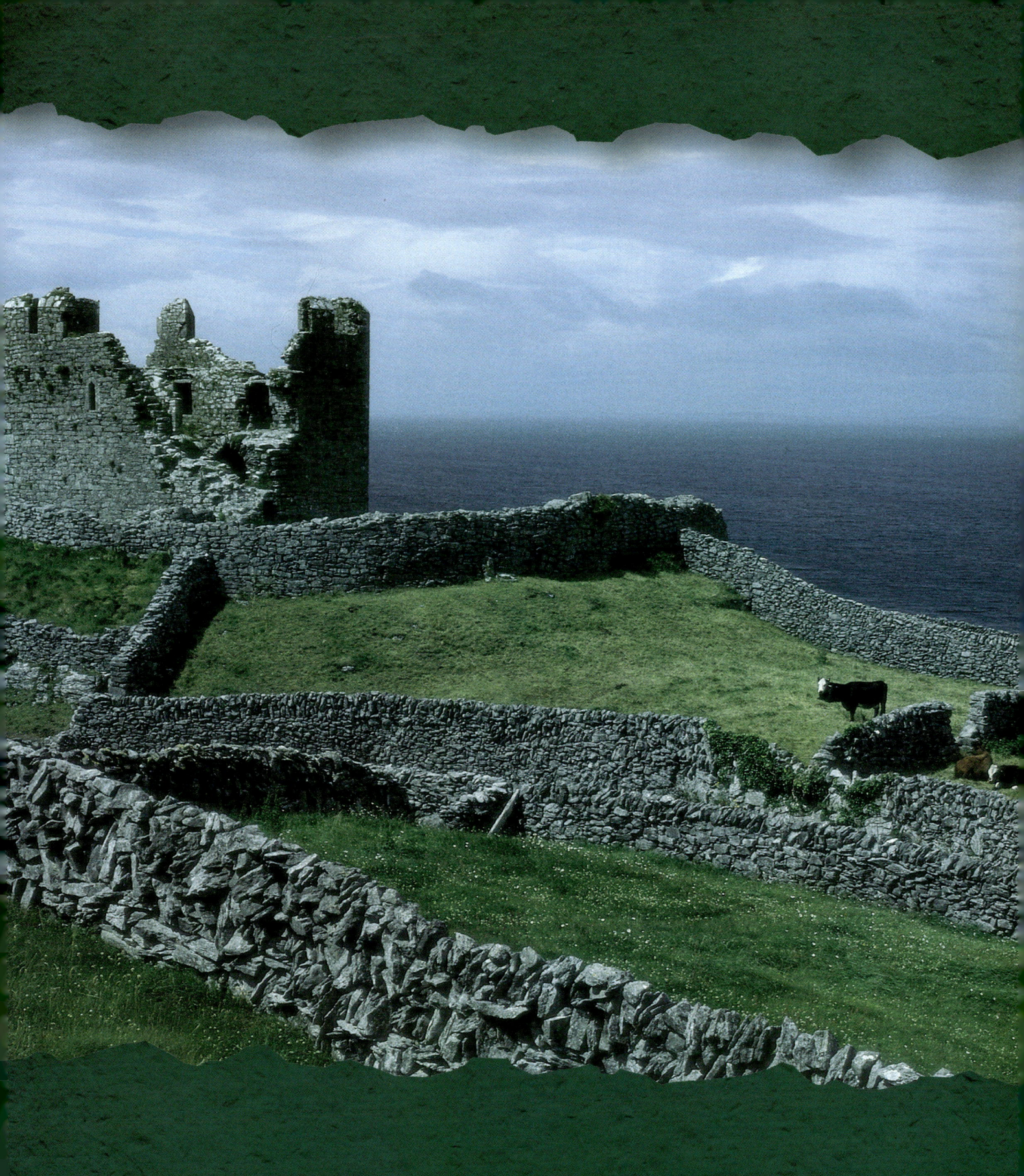

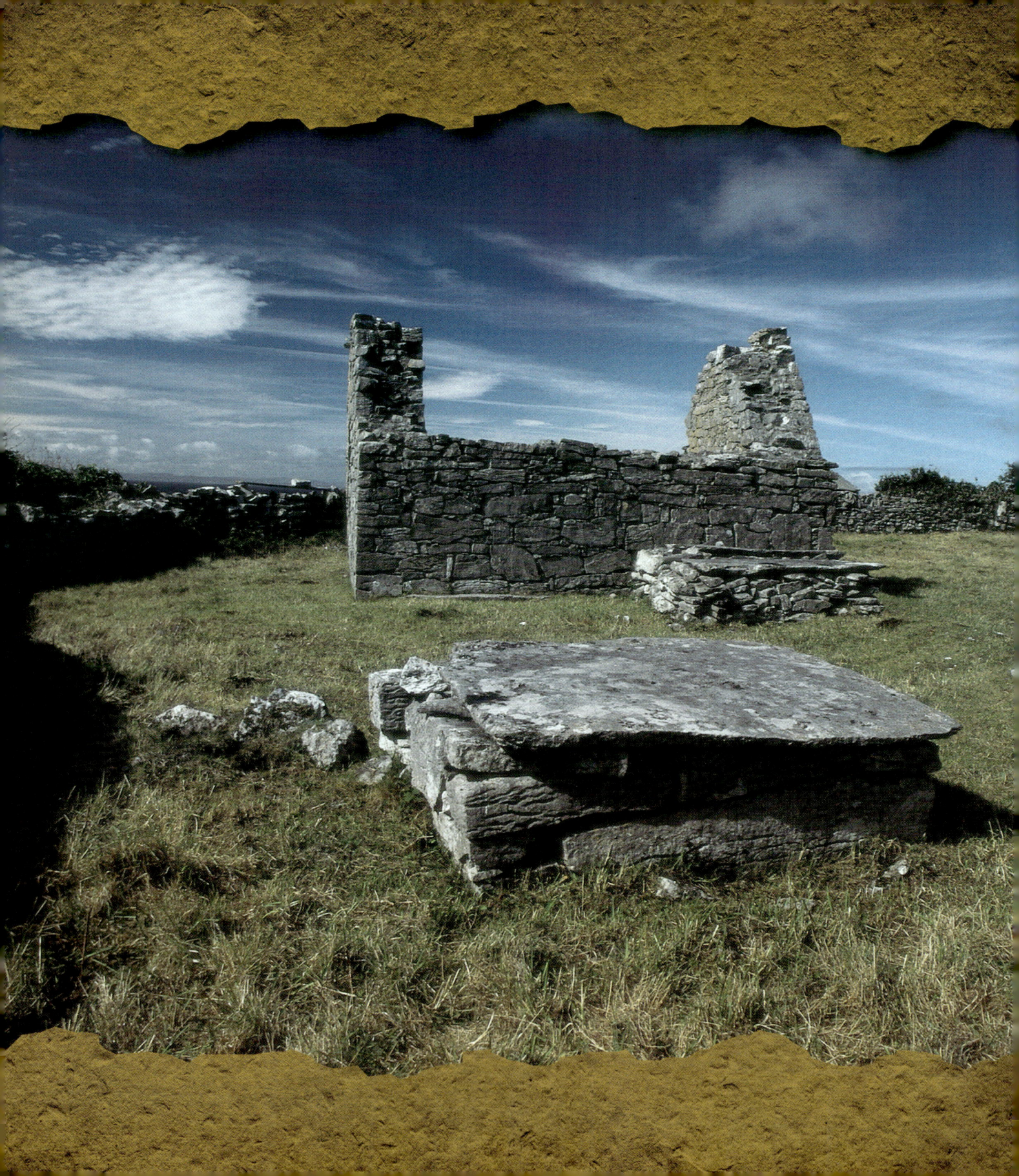

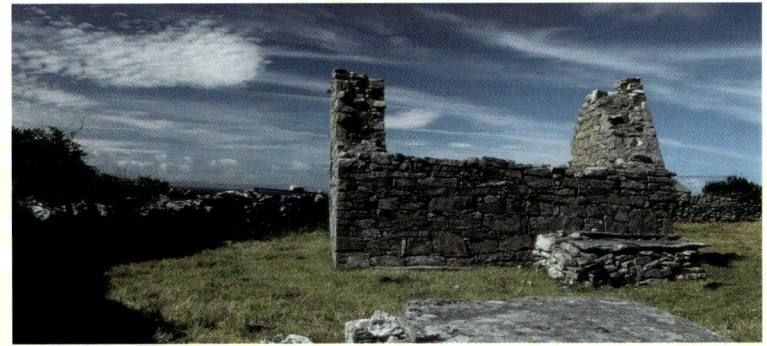

The Church of St. Ghobnait

St. Ghobnait has become known as the Patron Saint of Ballyvourney. A beekeeper by trade, she is also referred to as the Patron Saint of Beekeepers.

As the story goes, she had spent some time in West Clare at the Cliffs of Moher before fleeing to Inishere. From whom she was fleeing and why, remain a mystery, but it is said that she was a woman ahead of her time and therefore a threat to some. The escape route she followed was one she had seen in a vision.

Upon leaving Inishere, she finally settled in Ballyvourney, Co. Cork where she is commemorated on her Feast Day, the 11th of November.

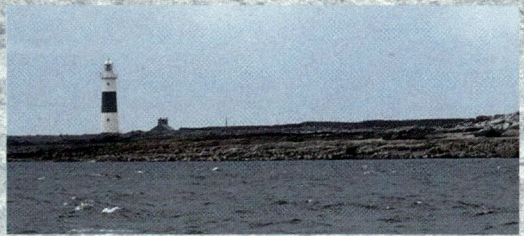

The Plassy Shipwreck

In 1950, a large cargo ship called the S.S. Plassy wrecked in the waters near Tra Caorach on Inishere. The entire crew was rescued by the islanders and eventually the strong seas carried the ship further ashore where it rests today.

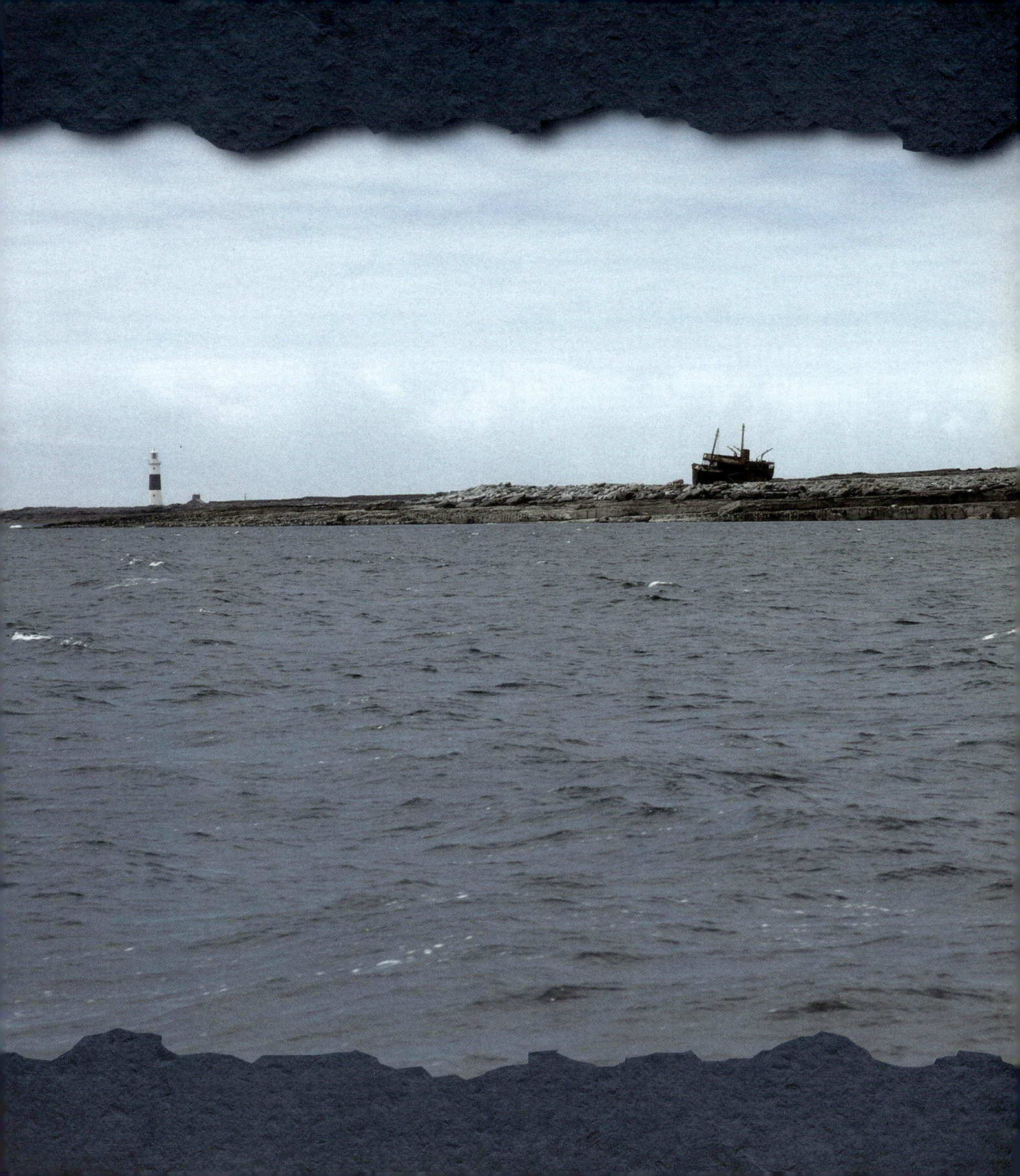

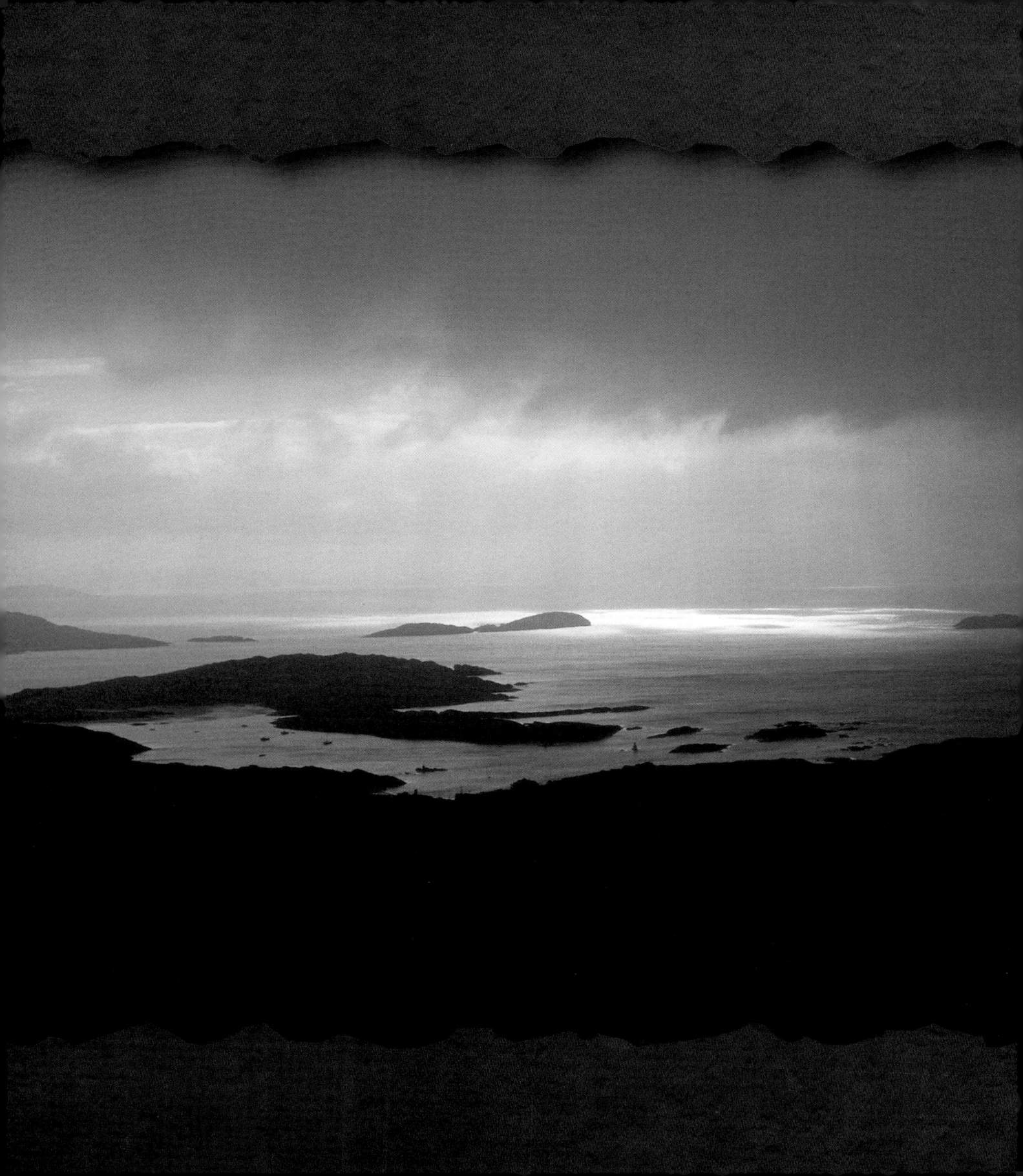

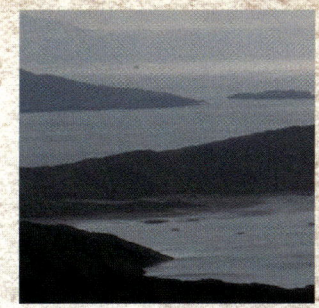

The Ring of Kerry

The Ring of Kerry is a scenic route that covers Co. Kerry's Iveragh peninsula. The circular route takes you through breathtaking mountain and coastal scenery, as well as woods, lakes and areas rich with historical monuments.

A view from the Ring of Kerry road between Waterville and Caherdaniel.

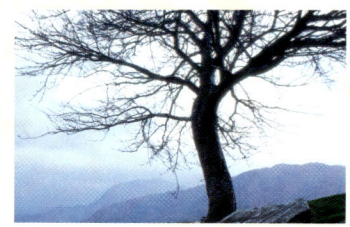

Ladies View

Continuing along the Ring of Kerry is a place called "Ladies View." The name commemorates an occasion over 100 years ago when Queen Victoria's ladies in waiting traveled here to admire the landscape.

"Ladies View" can be found along the Kenmare to Killarney Road. From here one can take in the entire Killarney valley including the Killarney lakes and the Gap of Dunloe.

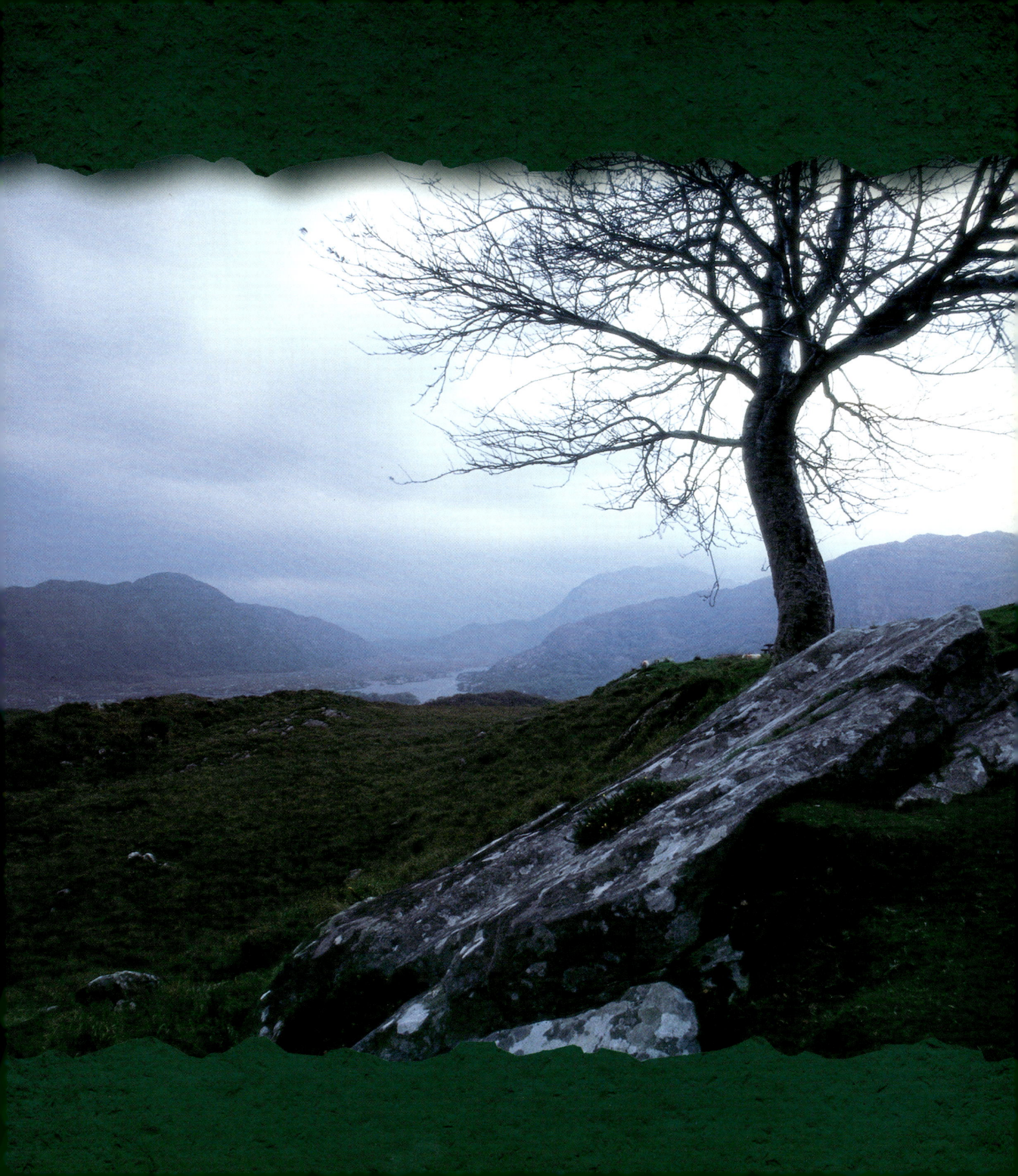

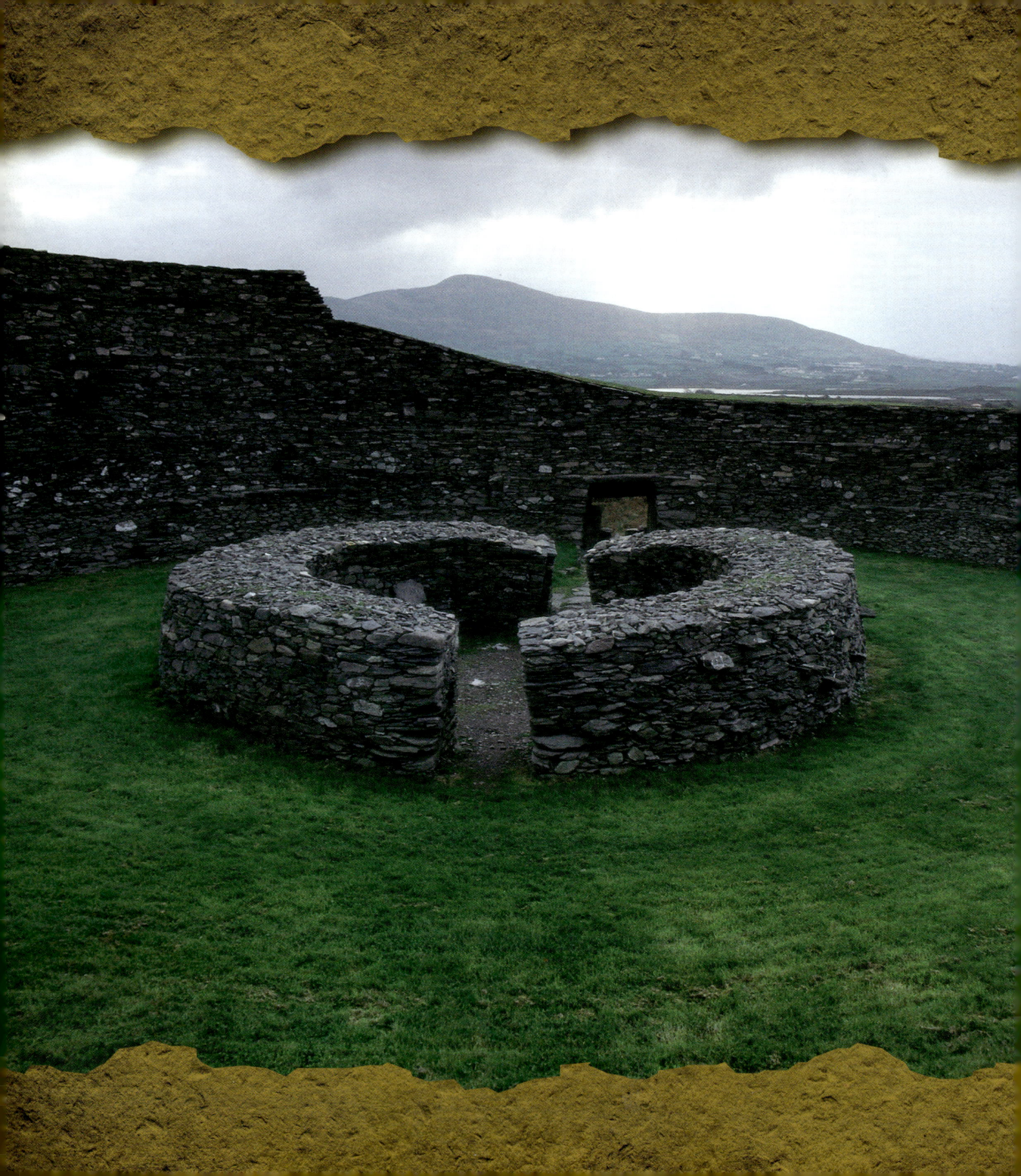

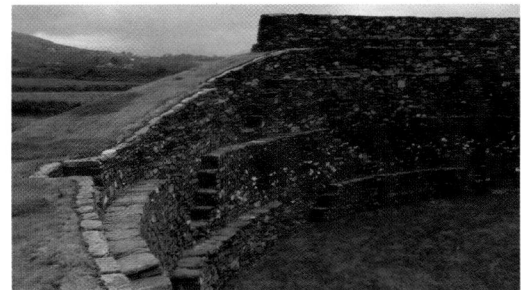

The Cahergall Ring Fort

During early times, the most common civilian settlement was the ring fort, also called a "Rath." These circular shelters provided sheep and cattle with protection from nocturnal predators. Most ring forts date from 500 - 1200 A.D. and were in use until the late 17th century.

This ring fort is called Cahergall and dates from the 9th century A.D. It is situated in Cahirciveen, Co. Kerry. Also shown are the stairs built into the wall from which the fort could be defended in time of attack.

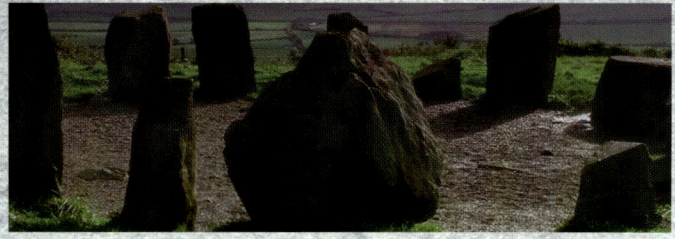

The Drombeg Stone Circle

There is a great deal of mystery and curiosity surrounding the existence of stone circles in Ireland. How the circles functioned in ancient times is not fully known. Part of their use was to serve as a calendar of sorts marking the time for spiritual celebration or ceremony. The Drombeg stone circle has a winter solstice sunset alignment. At the winter solstice (December 21, the shortest day of the year), the sun sets between a cleft in the hills to the west, shines over an axis stone (flat stone facing west), and through the entrance stones (tallest stones to the left).

The stones which make up the circle are sunk into the earth and held in place by "wedging" stones.

The Drombeg stone circle is believed to have been constructed between 4,000 and 5,000 years ago.

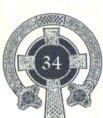

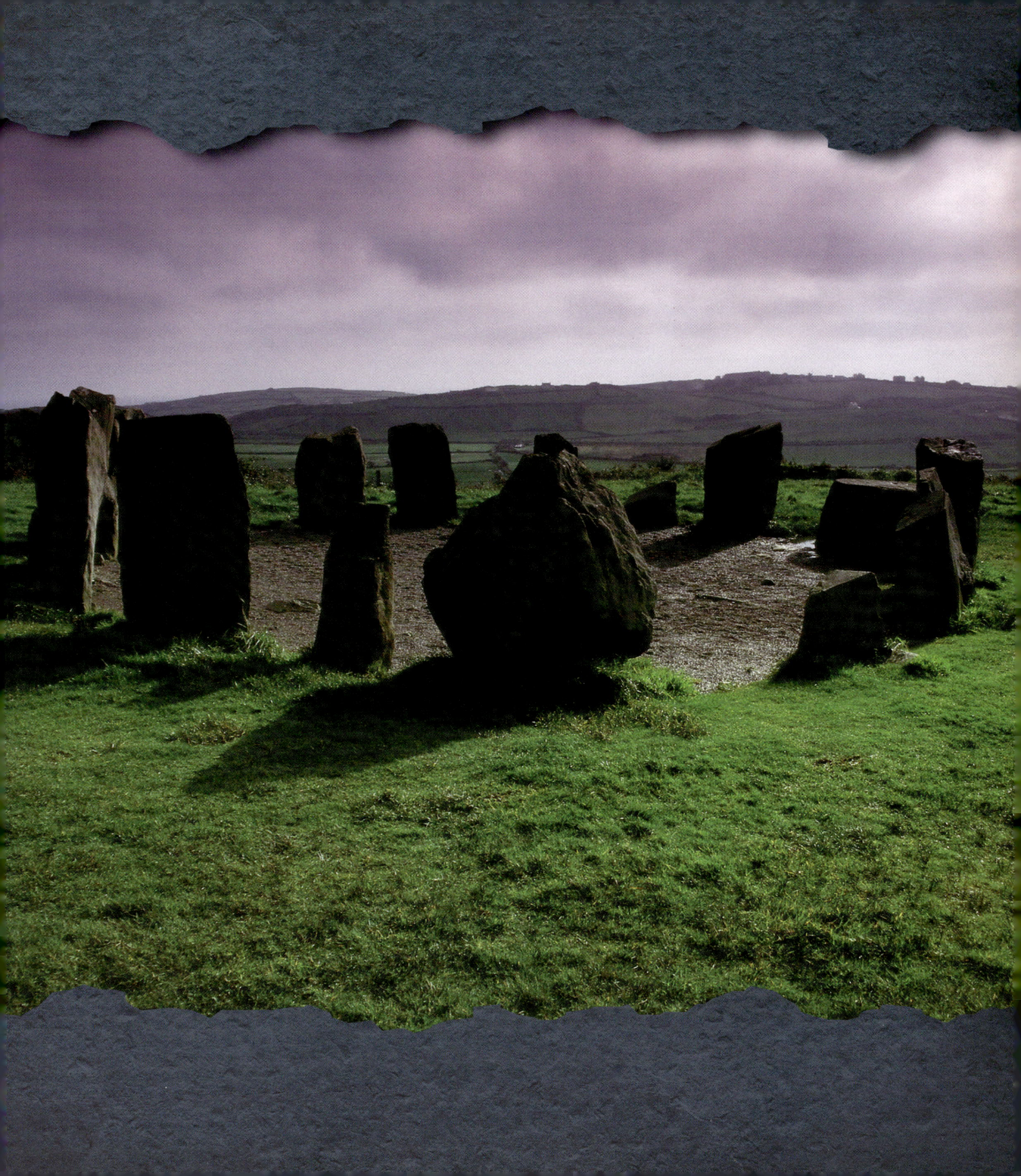

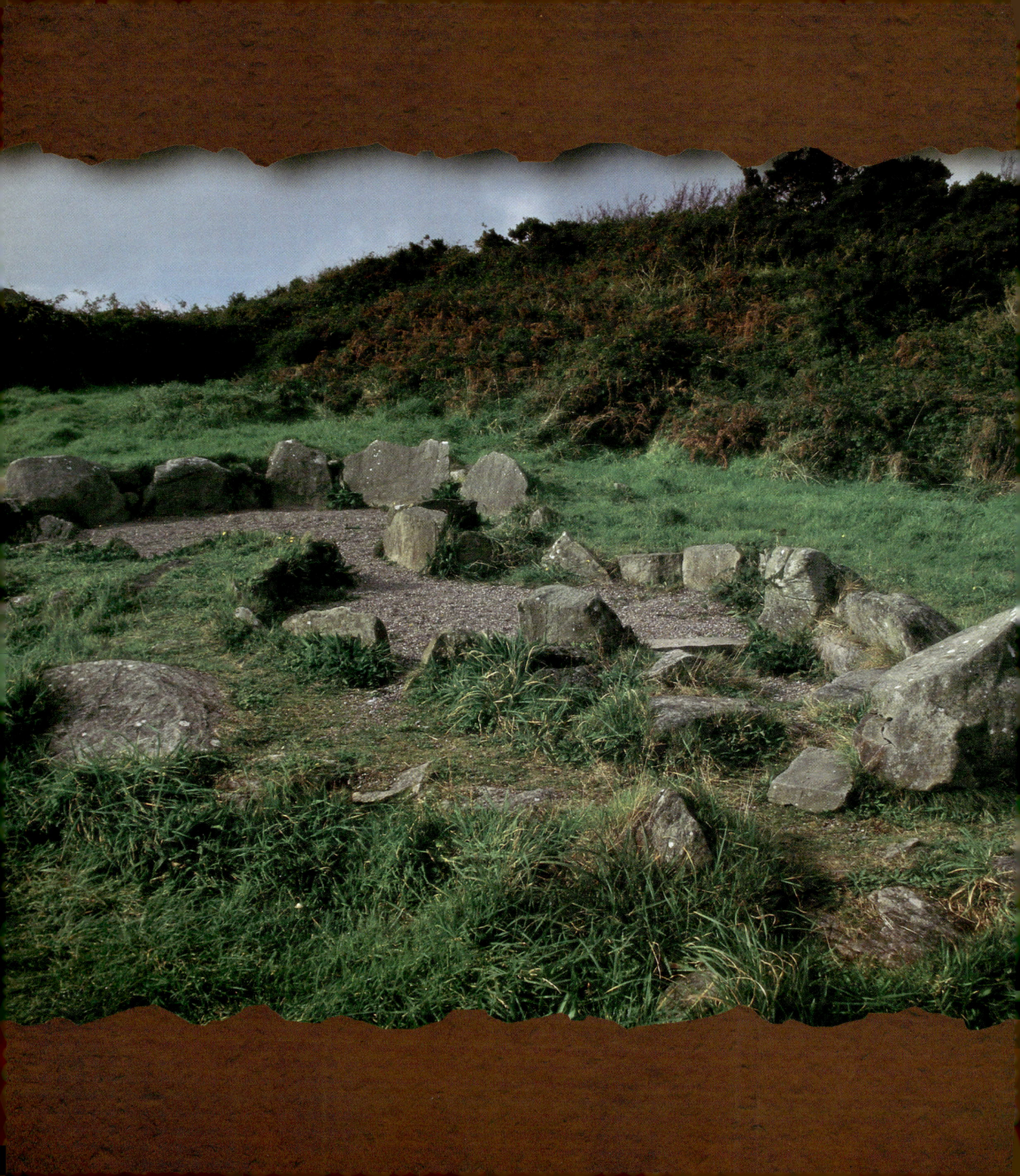

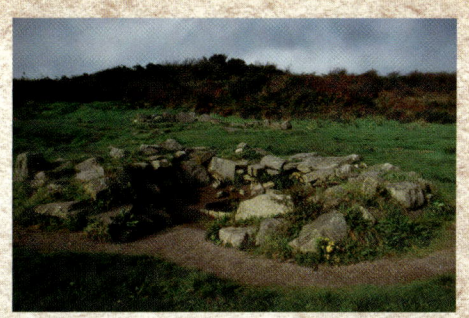

"Hut and Cooking Site"

Situated approximately 60 yards west of the Drombeg Stone Circle is a ruin known as a "hut site" where two round huts were joined together. This site dates to somewhere between 100 and 350 A.D.

Connected to the hut site by a stone causeway is another ruin called a "cooking place." In the center lies a water trough in which hot stones were placed to boil water. This site was constructed later, sometime between the middle 4th and early 7th centuries A.D.

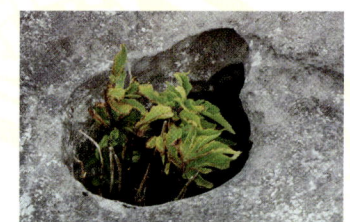

The Burren

There is a region in the middle west of Ireland known as the Burren. The name Burren means "Stoney place" which well describes the area with its lunar-like landscape consisting mainly of carboniferous limestone. The region also features caves and underground lakes.

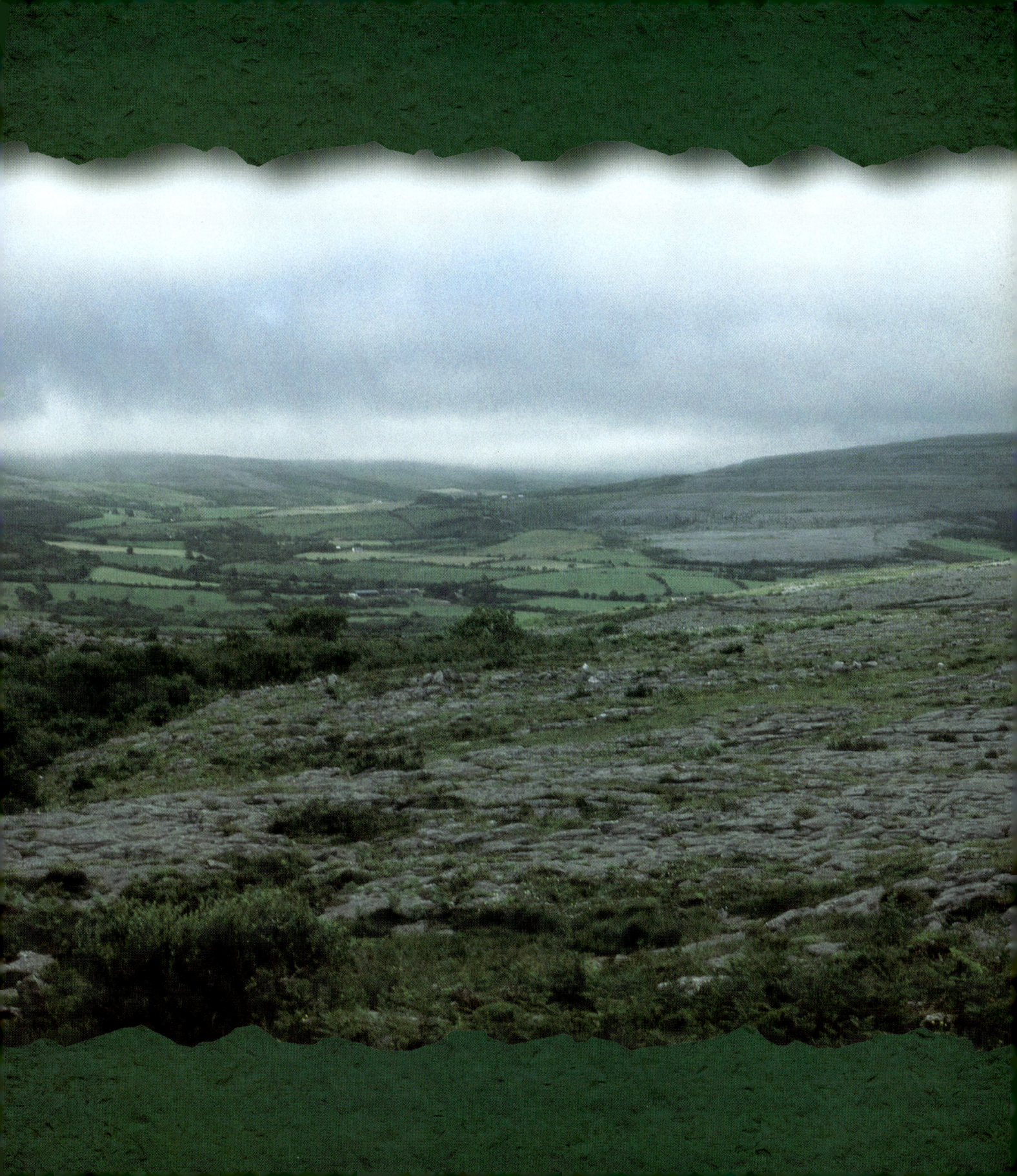

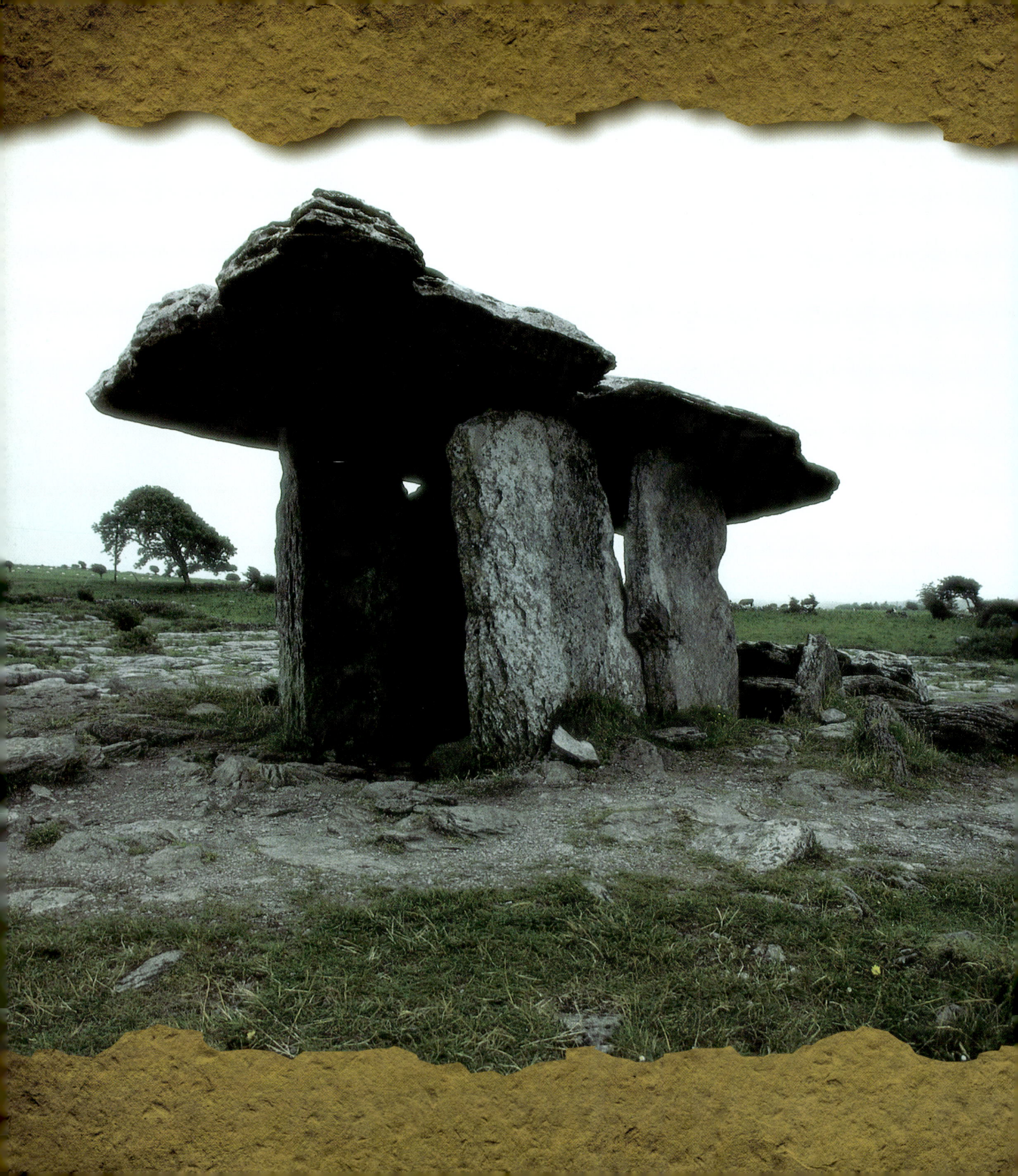

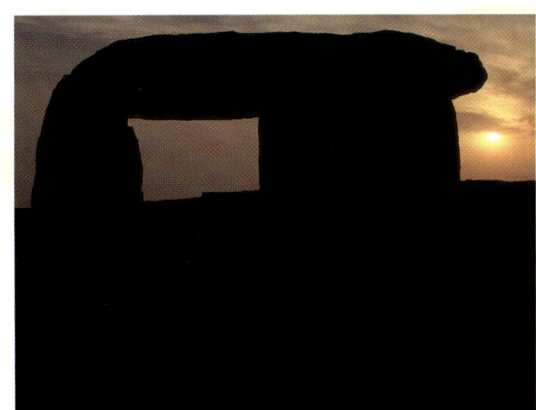

Dolmens

Also found in the Burren are many ancient monuments. These monuments show evidence of human habitation dating from 3,000 years B.C.

Noteworthy is the Poulnabrone Dolmen. The word "dolmen" is a derivative of a Breton word meaning "stone table" a name well suited to their appearance. At one time they were called "druids' altars." A more romantic eye saw dolmens as the "beds of Diarmuid and Gráinne," a mythic couple fleeing from a malevolent old King. The archeological explanation is that a dolmen is another example of a megalithic tomb used to mark the remains of ancestors. It is believed the dolmens were built between 3,000 - 2,000 B.C.

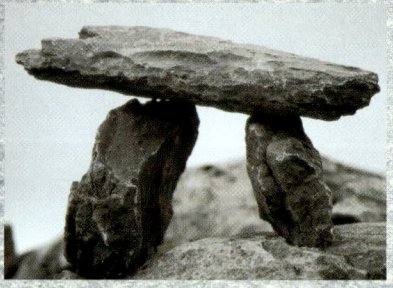

In Ruin Reconciled

I heard a woman's voice that wailed
    Between the sandhills and the sea:
The famished sea-bird past me sailed
    Into the dim infinity.

I stood on boundless, rainy moors:
    Far off I saw a great Rock loom;
The grey dawn smote its iron doors;
    And then I knew it was a Tomb.

Two queenly shapes before the grate
    Watched, couchant on the barren ground;
Two regal shapes in ruined state,
    One Gael, one Norman; both discrowned.

Aubrey De Vere
(1814-1902)

*These tiny dolmens scattered in a field are very close to the Poulnabrone Dolmen.
The miniatures stand only about one foot squared.*

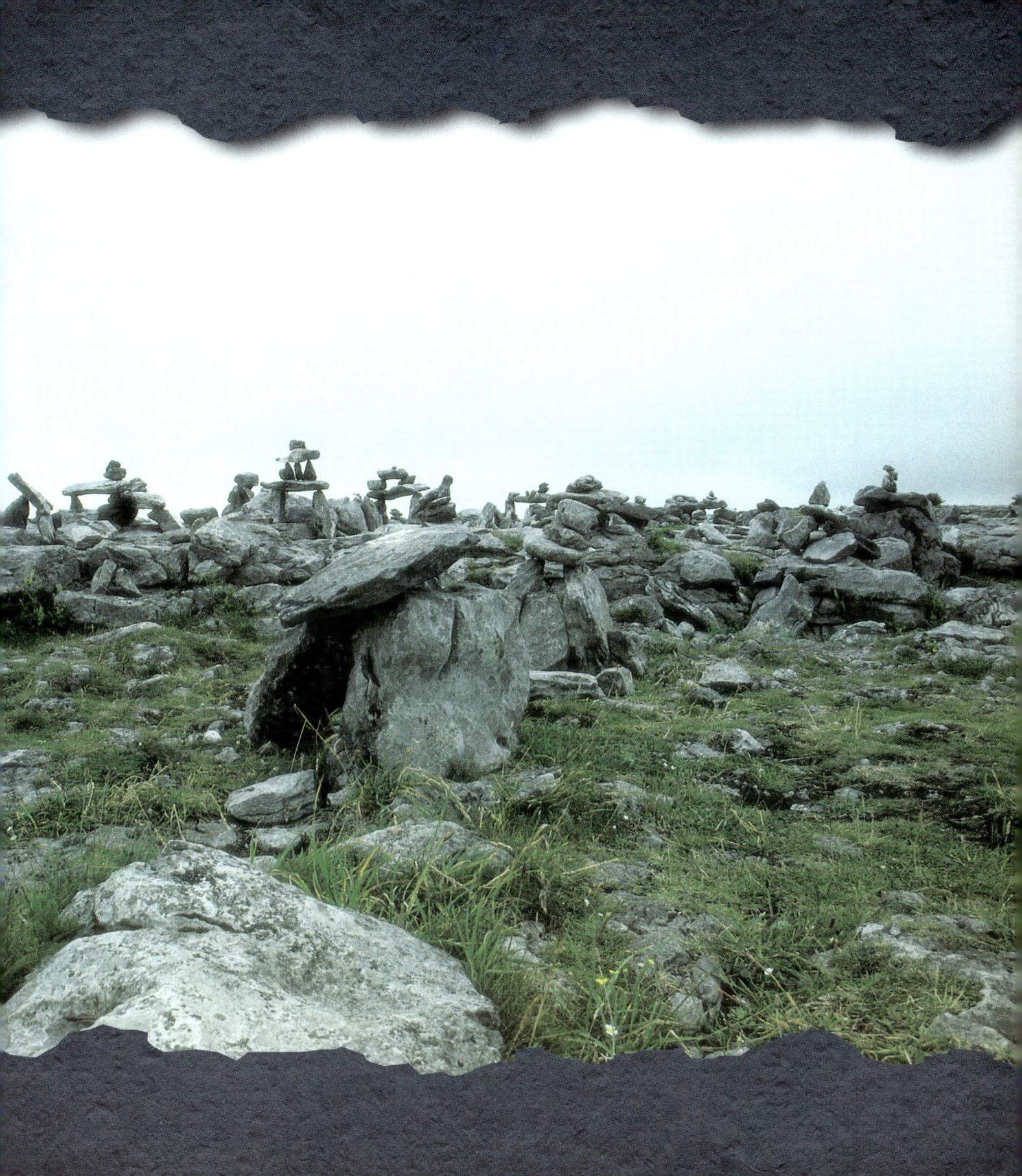

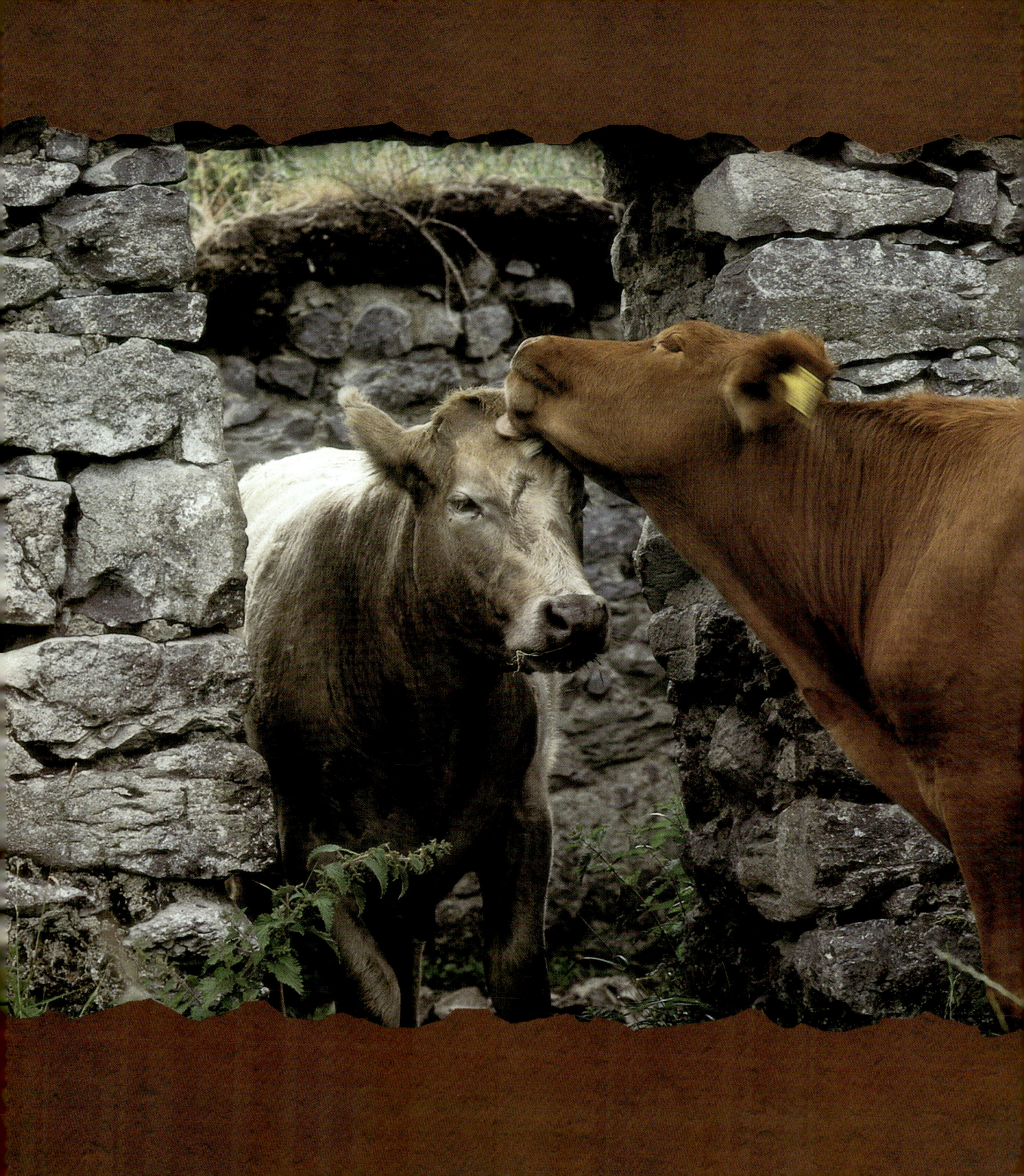

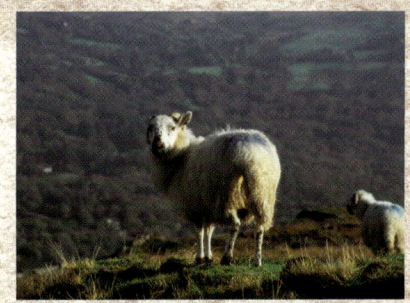

A Blessing For Animals

I say the blessing of Brighid
That she placed about her
calf and her cows,
About her horses and her goats,
About her sheep and her lambs:

Each day and night,
In cold and heat,
Each day and night,
In light and darkness:

Keep them from marsh,
Keep them from rocks,
Keep them from pits,
Keep them from banks;

Keep them from harm,
Keep them from jealousy,
Keep them from spell,
From North to South;

Keep them from poison,
From East and West,
Keep them from envy,
And from all harmful intentions.

from CARMINA GADELICA, VOL.4

Stone ruins in Kinvara, Co. Galway provide a home for cattle.
Sheep graze high on a hillside in scenic Glengarriff, Co. Cork.

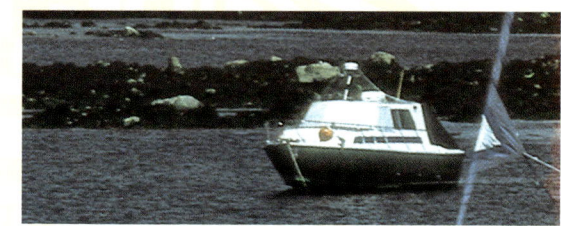

Roundstone Bay

Peacefully situated on the northwest coast of Co. Galway along Galway Bay is the small fishing village of Roundstone. The name Roundstone is an english derivation of Cloch na Ron, which means "Stone of the Seals".

The village was first settled in the early 19th century by Scottish fisherman, and by the 1840's, there were many making their living in the fishing trade.

The beauty of the area is represented in a number of major films including *Makintosh Man*, *Into the West* and *The Matchmaker*.

The mountain range known as the Twelve Pins can be seen in the distance.

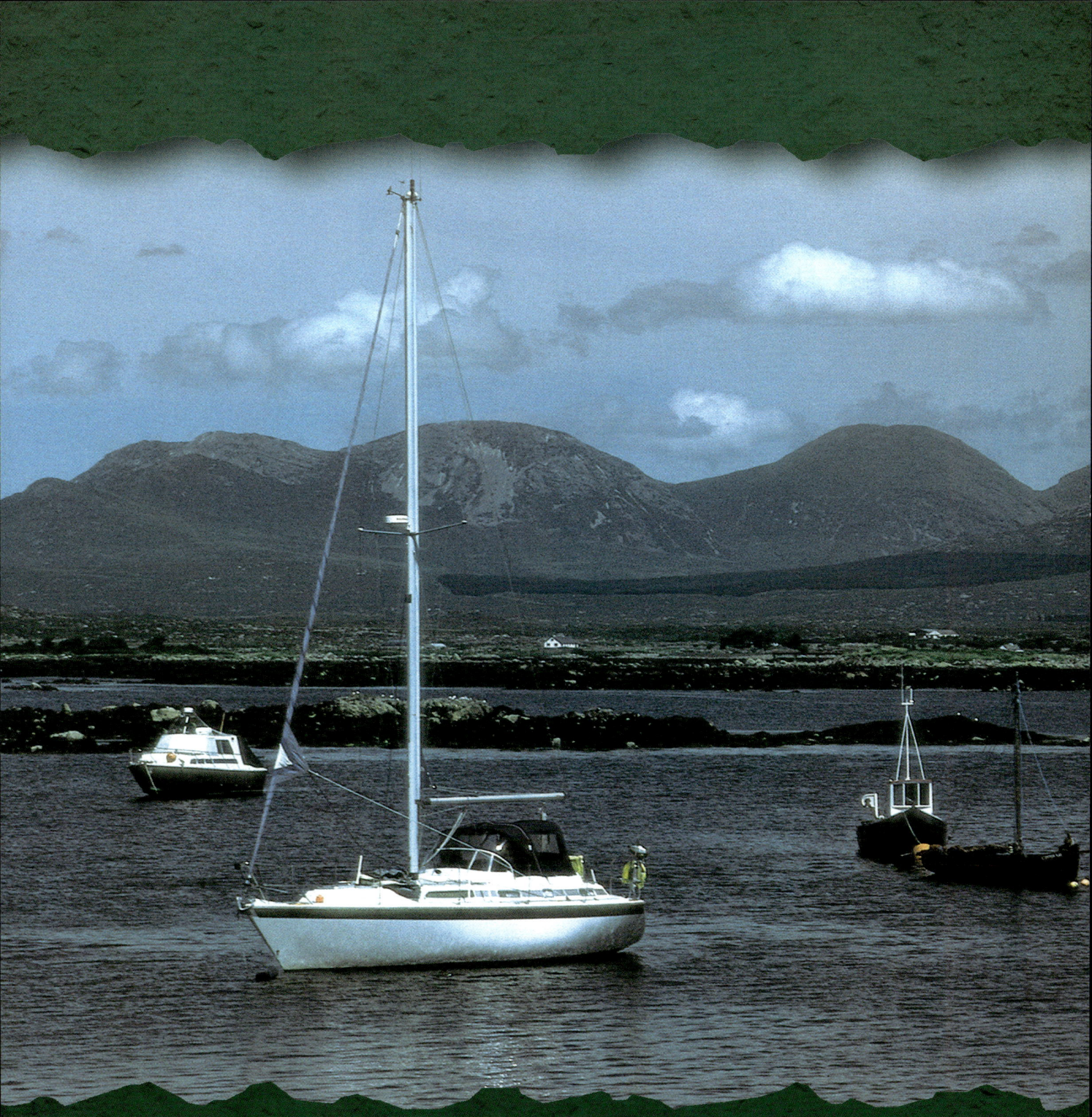

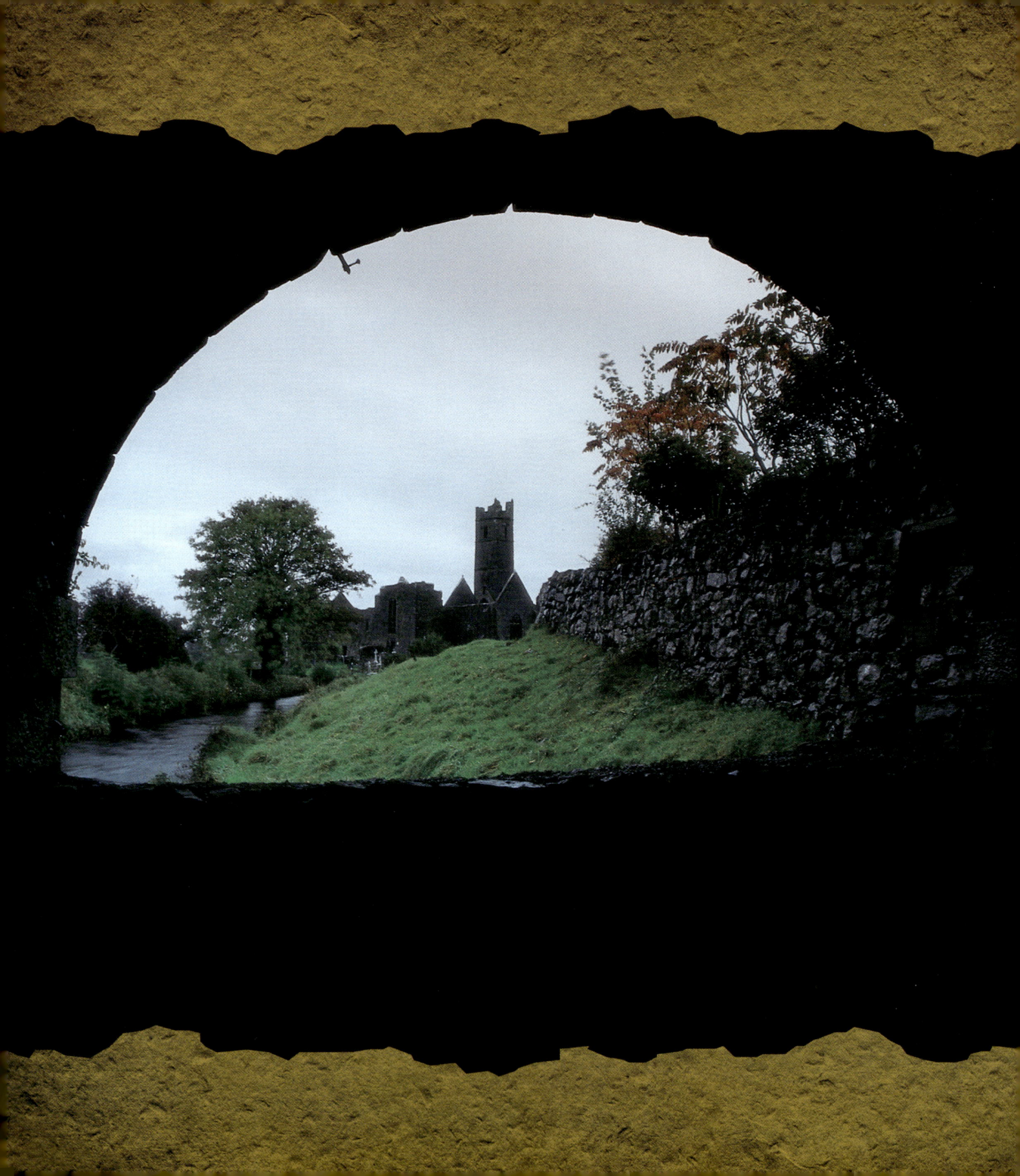

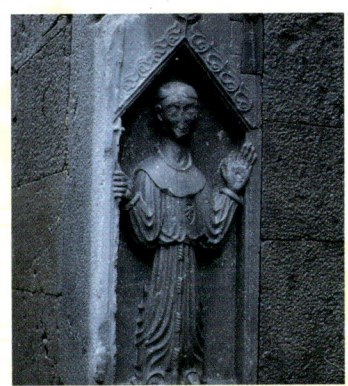

Love

Love bade me welcome; yet my soul drew back,
Guilty of dust and sin.
But quick-eyed Love, observing me grow slack
From my first entrance in,
Drew nearer to me, sweetly questioning
If I lacked anything.
"A guest," I answered, "worthy to be here:"
Love said, "You shall be he."
"I, the unkind, ungrateful? Ah, my dear,
I cannot look on Thee."
Love took my hand, and smiling did reply,
"Who made the eyes but I?"
"Truth, Lord, but I have marred them: let my shame
Go where it doth deserve."
"And know you not," says Love, "Who bore the blame?"
"My dear, then I will serve."
"You must sit down," says Love, "and taste my meat,"
So I did sit and eat.

George Herbert
(1593-1633)

The Franciscan abbey at Quin was built in 1433.

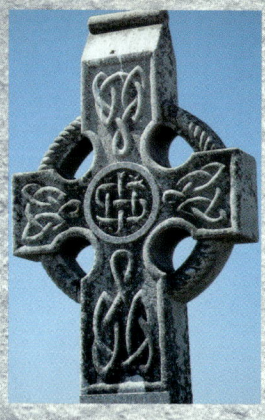

The Celtic Cross

The arrival of St. Patrick to Ireland brought about much change. Starting in the 6th and 7th centuries, a large number of monasteries blossomed throughout Ireland. These monasteries were important cultural centers as well as places of worship.

The earliest monasteries in Ireland were constructed primarily of wood. Most of the monasteries visible today, date from the 9th - 12th centuries, and the remains are of those structures that were made of stone.

The Celtic cross is defined by the circle at its center. There are three basic ideas as to the origin of its design, all of which probably played a part in its creation. One theory is that the cross symbolizes the unity of Christianity with the older Celtic religions with the circle representing the sun. Another possibility is that the ring represents the cosmos centering on the crucifixion. The third explanation, more architectural than spiritual, presumes that the circle would aid in supporting the heavy stone arms of these crosses.

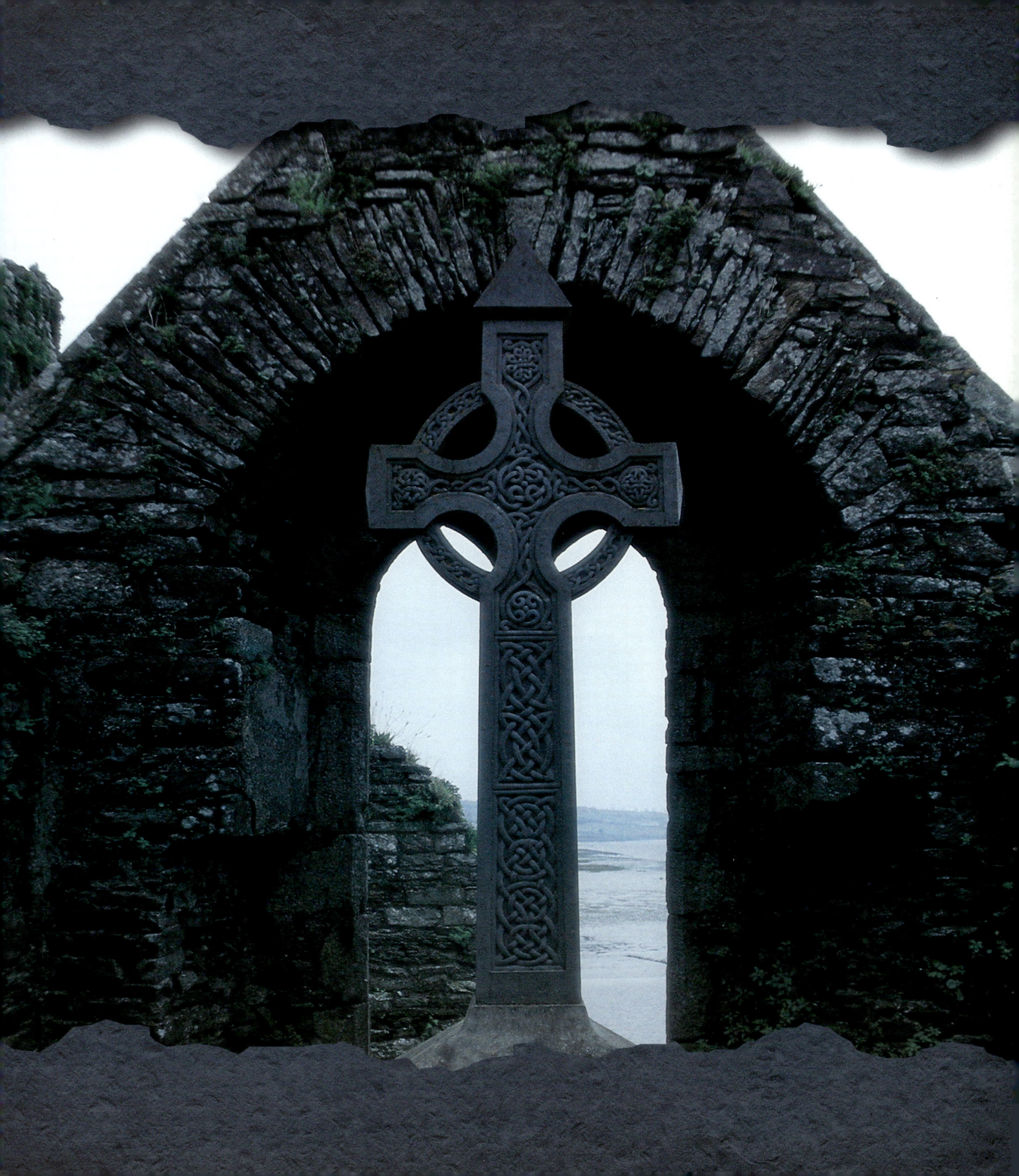

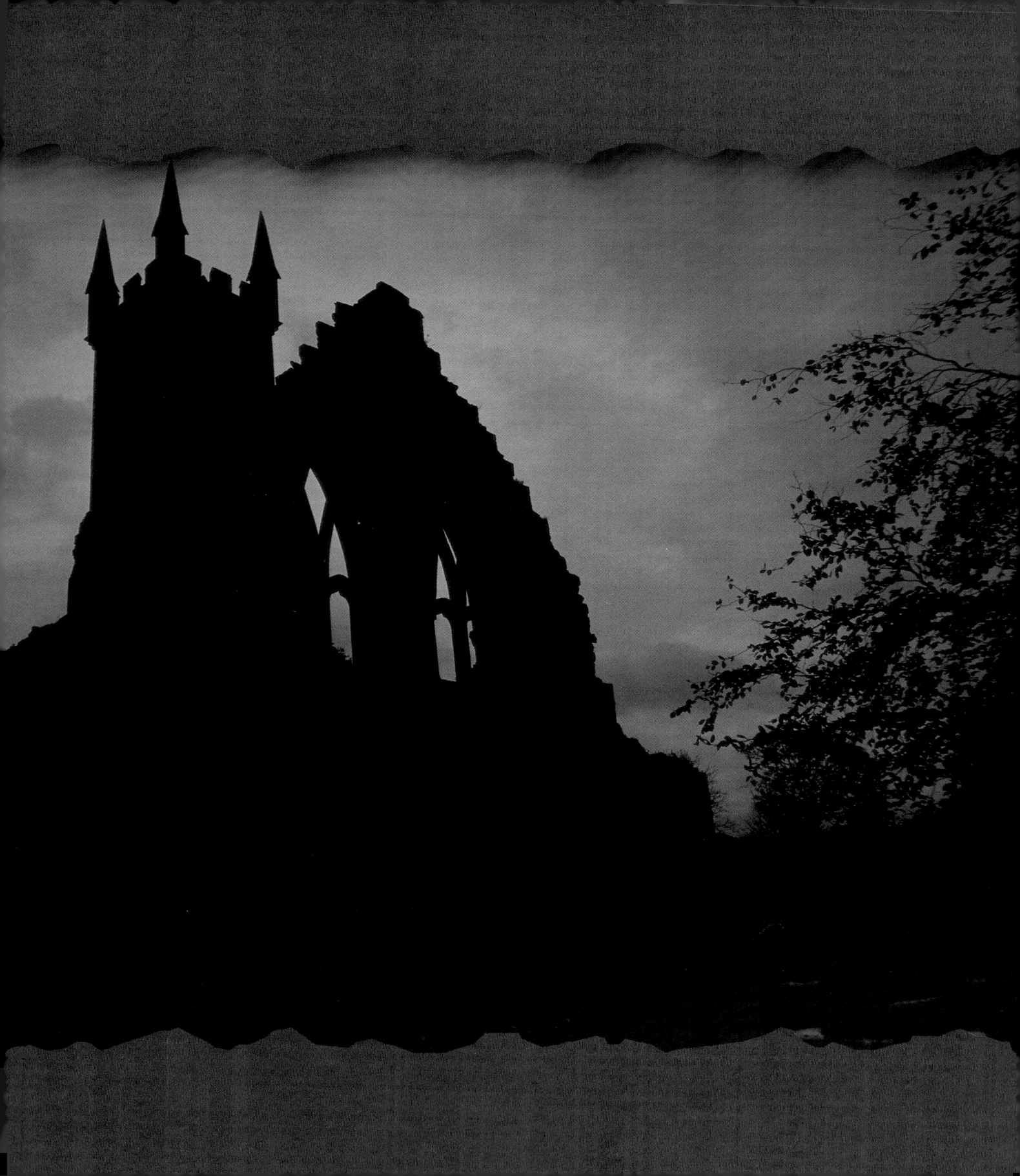

The Ennis Friary

The fall of the Roman Empire in the 5th century was marked with much violence and destruction. Since the reach of the Roman Empire never extended to Ireland, when the empire fell, Ireland was left unscathed. It was the monks in Ireland who were able to re-introduce the learning they had preserved, for the writings and teachings of their predecessors had not been destroyed.

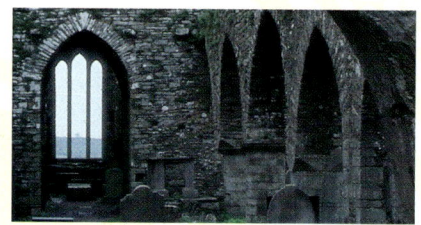

Franciscan Friary

It was in the 15th century that the Franciscans built their finest monasteries in Ireland. The current condition of these ruins is a testament to the quality of their workmanship.

This Franciscan Friary is in Timoleague, Co. Cork.

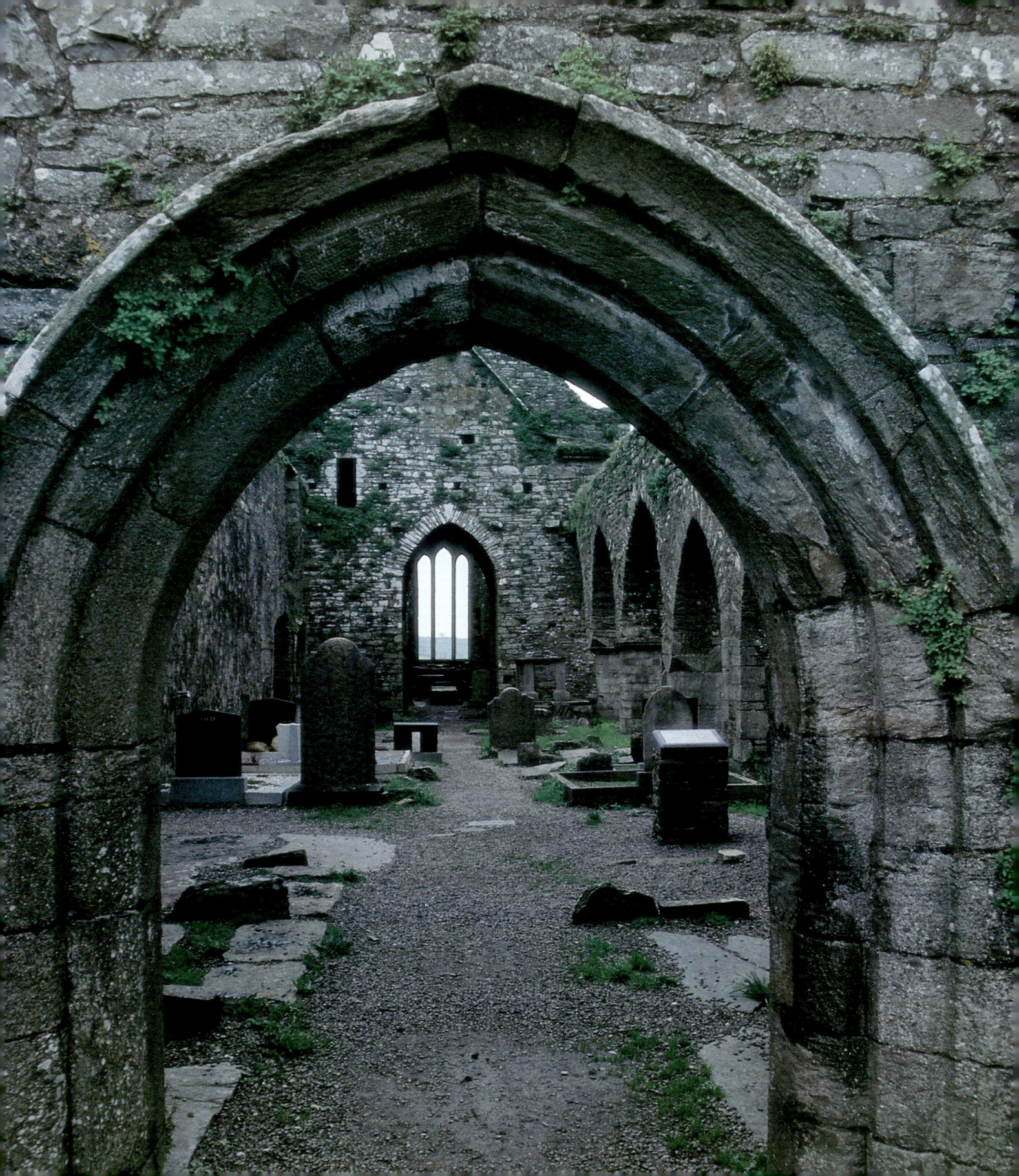

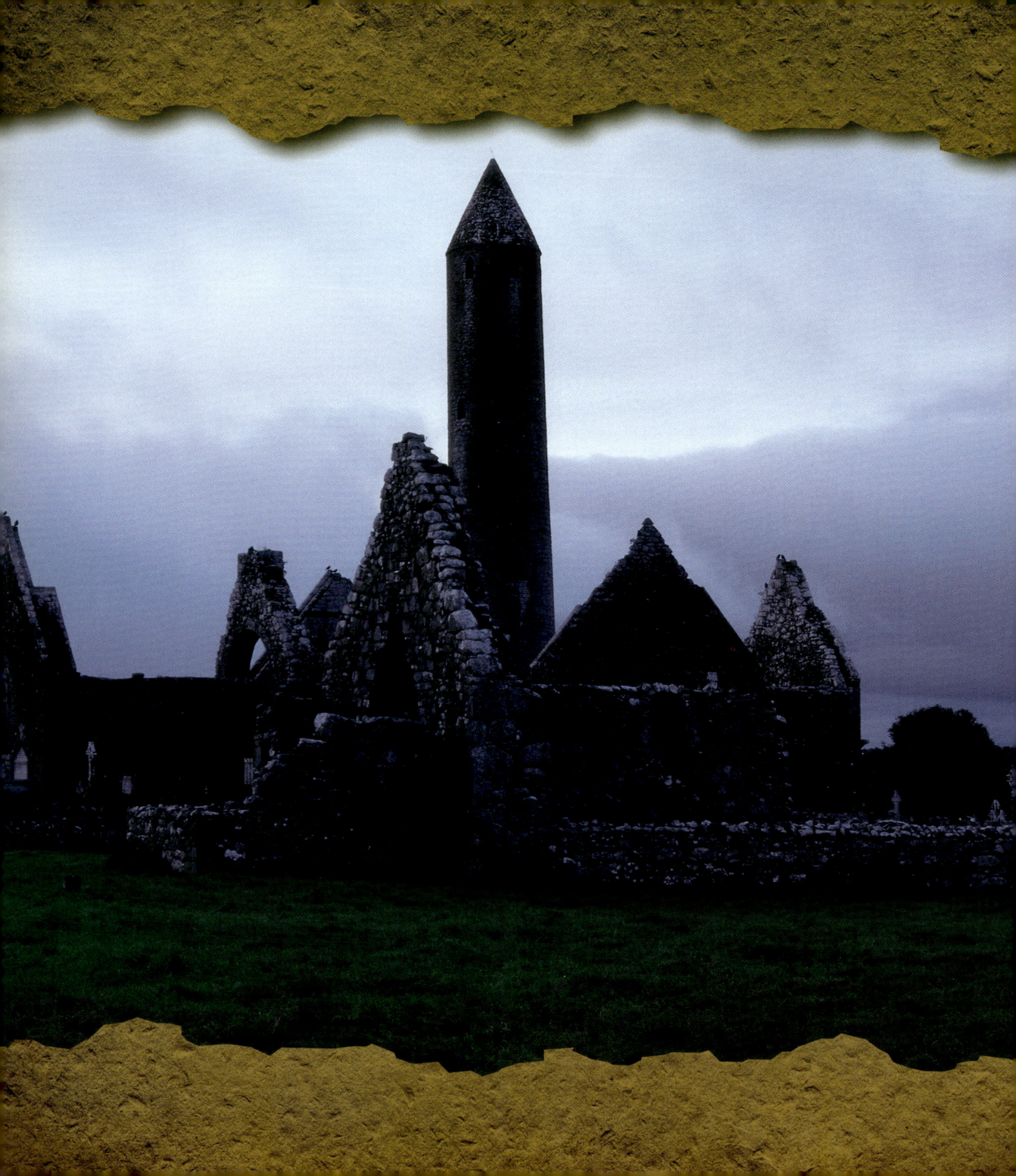

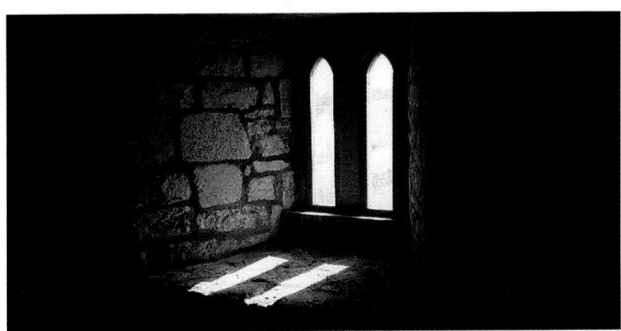

The Monastery at Kilmacduagh

The Kilmacduagh monastery was founded in the early 7th century by St. Colman. One of the finest in Ireland, it is situated in Co. Galway, just south of Kinvara.

Round towers in Ireland are said to have served several functions. Since the Irish word for the structure, "cloigtheach," means "bell tower," it may have been used as a lookout tower and a place from which to sound alarms in times of trouble. In peaceful times, the bells which rang from it probably called the members of the monastery to their meals and other daily duties. As its height made it visible from great distance, it may have also served as a beacon guiding weary travelers to its safe haven. Another function would have been the storage of monastic treasures, as well as a hiding place for the monks themselves, during attack. Many of the doorways to these towers are ten to twelve feet off the ground and the monks were able to climb up to the tower door and then draw the ladder up behind them.

This round tower at Kilmacduagh dates from the 12th century and leans two feet out perpendicular.

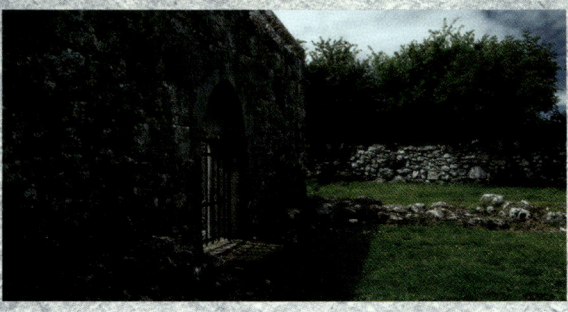

Invocation

Open me the way that to the City bright
Leads forth; let Thy Word's lamp be light
To guide my footsteps through the narrow gate,
Where the Good Shepherd feeds His sheep, elate:
There first the Virgin's white lamb entered
And all His fair flock followed where He led!
With Thee how smooth the way: for Nature all
Thine empire owns! Thou speakest, her fetters fall
And all her wonted shows new forms assume:
The frozen fields will into verdure bloom
And winter gild with grain: if Thou but will
'Mid budding Spring the swelling grape shall fill,
And sudden labor tread the bursting vine.
All seasons answer to the call Divine!

Caelius Sedulius,
(Irish bard ca. 5th century)

O'Heyne's Church at Kilmacdaugh was built in the early part of the 13th century.

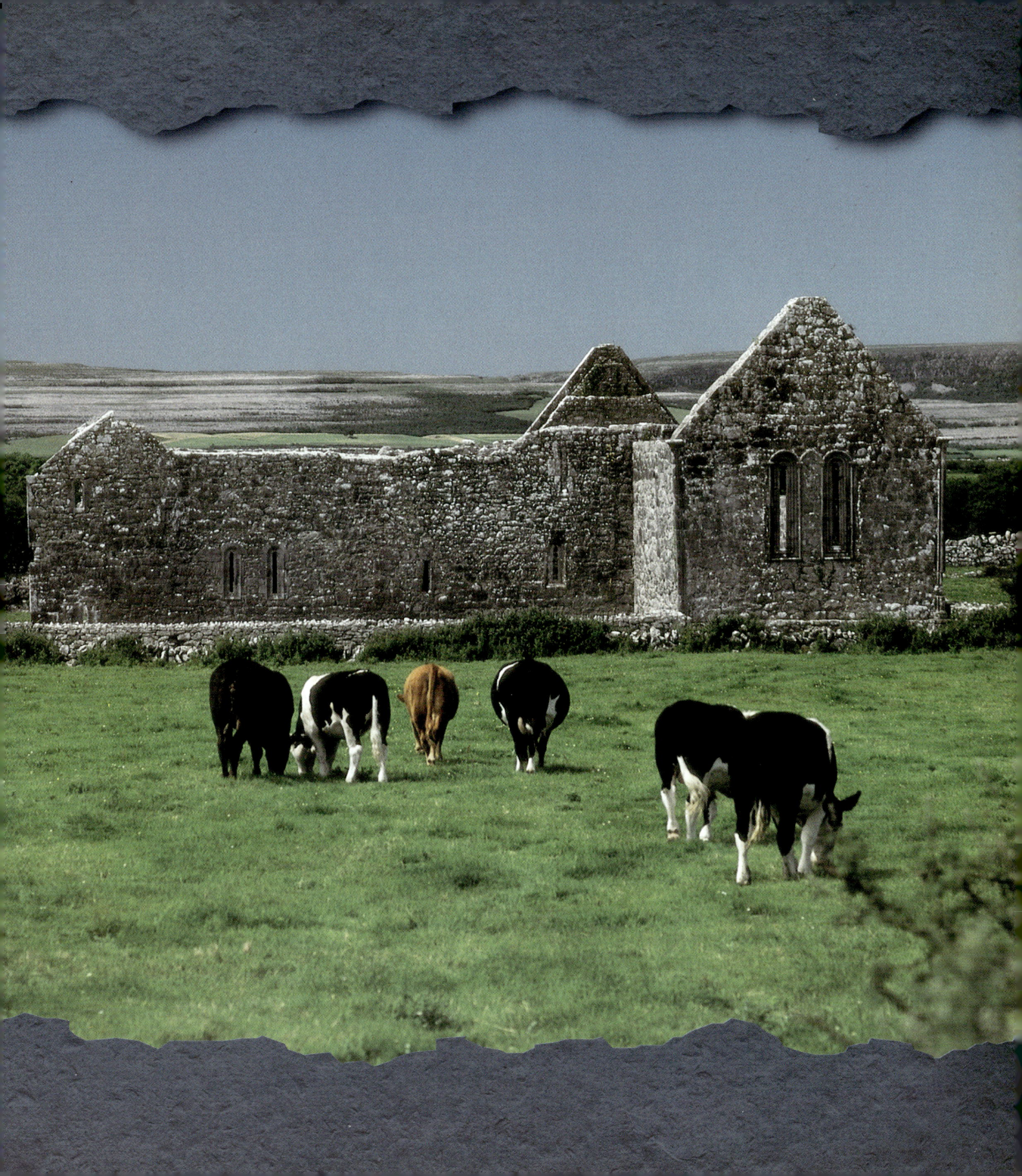

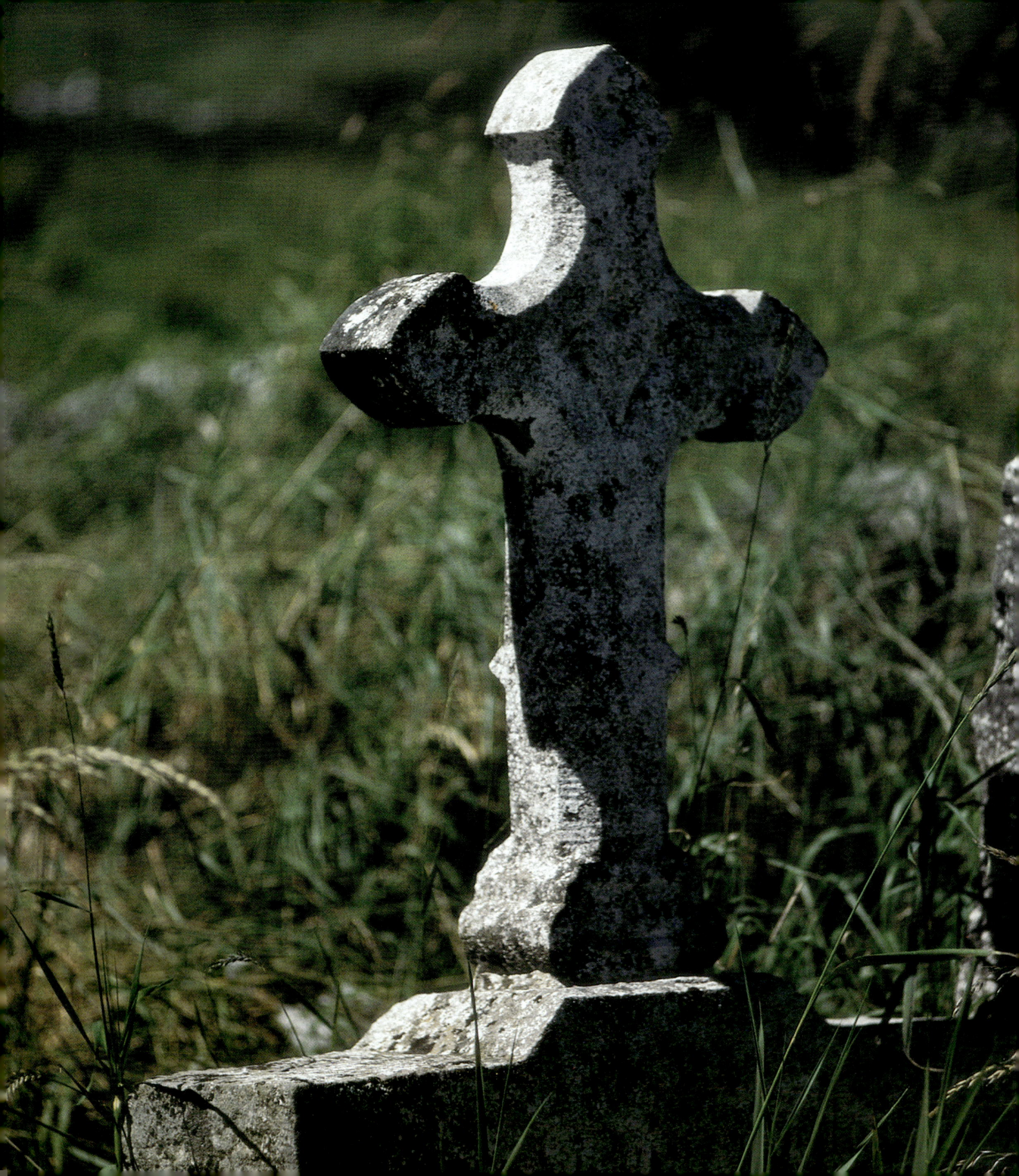

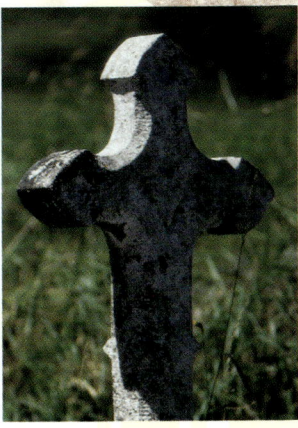

Rest Only In The Grave

I rode till I reached the House of Wealth -
'Twas filled with riot and blighted health.

I rode till I reached the House of Love -
'Twas vocal with sighs beneath and above!

I rode till I reached the House of Sin -
There were shrieks and curses without and within.

I rode till I reached the House of Toil -
Its inmates had nothing to bake or boil.

I rode in search of the House of Content
But never could reach it, far as I went!

The House of Quiet, for strong and weak
And poor and rich, I have still to seek -

That House is narrow, and dark, and small
But the only Peaceful House of all.

James Clarence Mangan
(1803-1849)

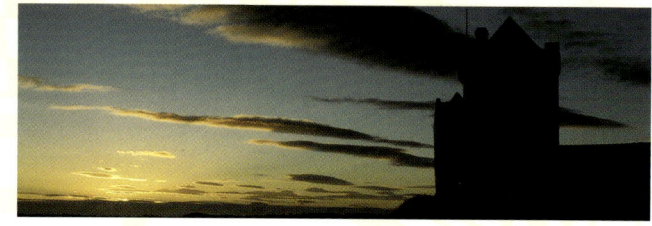

Ireland

I called you by sweet names by wood and linn,
You answered not because my voice was new,
And you were listening for the hounds of Finn
And the long hosts of Lugh.

And so, I came unto a windy height
And cried my sorrow, but you heard no wind,
For you were listening to small ships in flight,
And the wail on hills behind.

And then I left you, wandering the war
Armed with will, from distant goal to goal,
To find you at the last free as of yore,
Or die to save your soul.

And then you called to us from far and near
To bring your crown from out the deeps of time,
It is my grief your voice I couldn't hear
In such a distant clime.

Francis Ledwidge
(1891-1917)

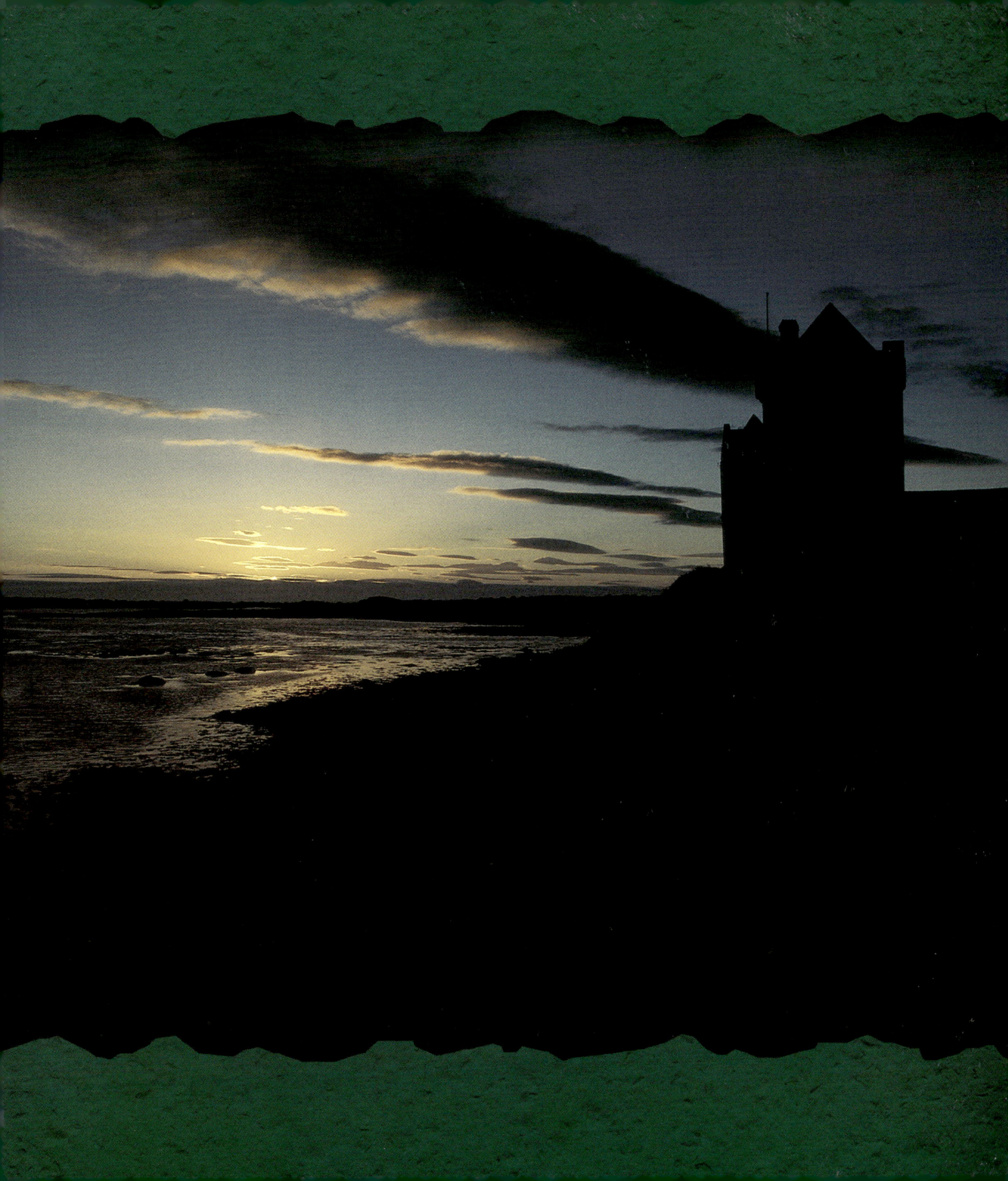

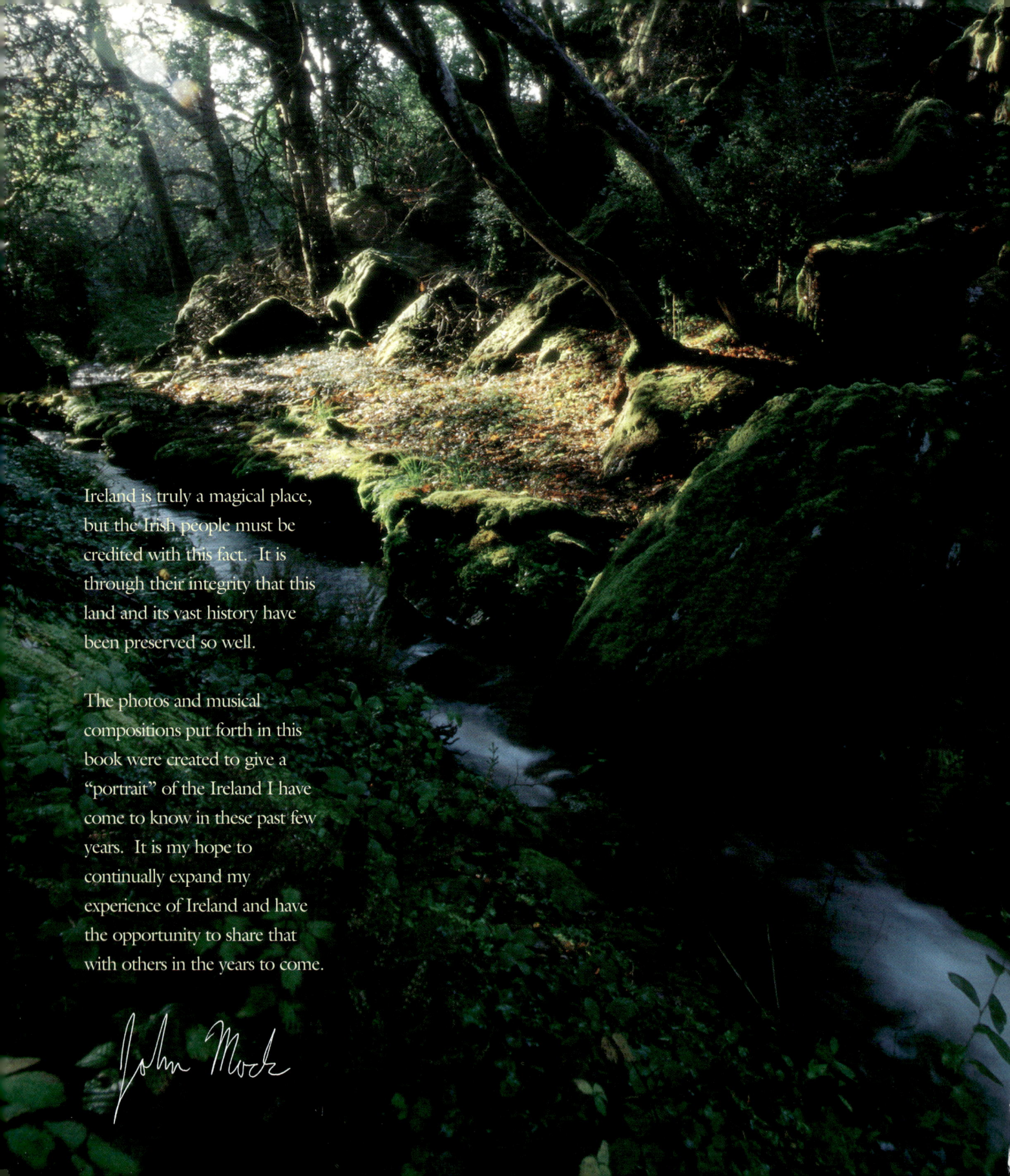

Ireland is truly a magical place, but the Irish people must be credited with this fact. It is through their integrity that this land and its vast history have been preserved so well.

The photos and musical compositions put forth in this book were created to give a "portrait" of the Ireland I have come to know in these past few years. It is my hope to continually expand my experience of Ireland and have the opportunity to share that with others in the years to come.

John Mock

Special Thanks

*To Lee Satterfield, Sylvia Hutton,
Roy Hutton and Peter Cairney for their
inspiration and help with editing*

*This book is lovingly dedicated to Maggie.
We miss you.*